STORAGE

Creative Solutions for a Well-Organised Home

CAROLINE CLIFTON-MOGG

jacqui small

First published in 2007 by Jacqui Small LLP,
an imprint of Aurum Books, 25 Bedford Avenue, London WC1B 3AT

Text copyright © Caroline Clifton-Mogg 2007
Photography, design and layout copyright © Jacqui Small 2007

The author's moral rights have been asserted.

PUBLISHER Jacqui Small
EDITORIAL MANAGER Kate John
DESIGNER Ashley Western
EDITOR Hilary Mandleberg
PRODUCTION Peter Colley
PICTURE RESEARCH Nadine Bazar

ISBN-13: 978 1 903221 71 6

A catalogue record for this book is available from the British Library.

2008 2007 2006
10 9 8 7 6 5 4 3 2 1

Printed in China

contents

Introduction 6

WHY HAVE STORAGE? 8

ACTION PLAN 26
What are you storing? 30
Ways to store 36

WHAT GOES WHERE? 74
Living rooms 78
Kitchens 92
Somewhere to eat 102
Hallways and stairs 110
Bedrooms 114
Bathrooms 124
Home office 130
Utility rooms 134

Suppliers 136
Architects & Designers 139
Acknowledgements 142

These days, storage is big consumer business and over the last few years numerous outlets have sprung up to offer us a huge range of choice. From department stores to small specialist shops and from mail-order catalogues and on-line shopping, 'storage solutions' leap at you from every corner. It's all very seductive.

But beware! Before you start thinking about what sort of storage you want, I would like to offer a word of warning. However ingenious, good-looking or adaptable a piece of storage furniture seems to be in the shop or catalogue, believe me, it really is far better not to buy without doing your homework. You know what happens if you don't. You see something that catches your eye and immediately you are sure it will cater for your every storage need – as well as for needs you haven't yet dreamt of. Then you get it home and ... it doesn't quite make the grade. You are stuck with what might well be an expensive mistake. This book is intended to help you avoid the pitfalls. I hope it does.

Caroline Clifton-Mogg

RIGHT A traditional way of decorating simple shelves is to add trimming to the front edge – either of paper or fabric.

FAR RIGHT Everyone has need of those small, but always useful storage containers that can range from woven baskets, as seen here, with little identification tags, to tins, boxes and bags.

THIS PAGE In a country kitchen, a most traditional form of storage is one that runs the length of the wall and comprises deep shelves of varying heights; here, the recessed lights add a modern touch.

Why have storage?

THIS PAGE A wall of unobtrusive storage provides the perfect home for a large book collection: it proves that well-planned storage encourages a sense of tidiness and efficiency as well as being pleasing to look at.

Asking 'Why have storage?' seems at first to be one of those questions to which the answer is blindingly obvious. What could be simpler? We need it to house our possessions – all the things which are necessary for our busy, complicated lives. But why should you store it all rather than just leave it lying around in piles or pushed under the nearest bed? The answer will become clear as you read the following pages, but it can be summed up in just a few words: tidiness, efficiency, pleasure, cleanliness and safety. But first things first. Look around you and ask yourself, is everything that you see totally necessary? If you were to open that cupboard does it only contain things you really need? If you answer 'no', your first step is to get rid of anything you don't use any more. Just as every fashion writer exhorts us to get rid of clothes that we haven't worn for a year, so we should purge our other possessions with the same detachment. Your clutter will instantly be reduced and so will your storage problem. Make your mantra 'sort and eliminate'. I promise that it will make you feel much better and once you have sorted and eliminated, you will be ready to think in greater depth about how to store what is left. And now, let's see why it is all going to be worth the bother.

TOP LEFT The upward-opening door is both space-saving and visually attractive; it is secured by a regulated hinge mechanism that holds the door partially open.

TOP RIGHT Individual figured-wood storage boxes are ranged along a wall, connected by a sculptural, curved, 'floating' shelf.

CENTRE LEFT A deep-shelved traditional cupboard is the perfect place for storing china; here old and new pieces are combined in functional groups, united by shape.

CENTRE RIGHT On an airy landing the bulk of a heavy, bold wood and glass catch-all bookcase is balanced by being set between two tall windows and a pair of chairs.

BOTTOM LEFT An oversized clothes cupboard, painted the same colour as the room, has the surprising effect of making the space seem larger rather than smaller.

BOTTOM RIGHT A metal cupboard that once had another use altogether, now makes a perfect store for a collection of old, hand-painted faïence pieces.

TIDINESS AND EFFICIENCY

BELOW LEFT A half-seen display of clothes stored in a dressing room makes for an ever-changing coloured backdrop to enliven the adjoining all-white kitchen.

BELOW RIGHT A practical and comprehensive wall of storage is divided into units of different sizes whose flat-fronted doors add a sculptural touch.

Well-planned storage is more, much more, than a means of keeping things tidy and of banishing clutter. It brings order into your life and will make it easy to manage – enjoyable even – in a way that it never could be in cluttered, haphazard circumstances. Well-planned storage makes for a tidy home and is essential to the running of an efficient life – which is something we all aspire to, even if only spasmodically.

Have you never gone hunting for one specific item at home and experienced that sense of rising panic as you look around you, noticing precipitous piles of floor-bound paper or chairs decked out like miniature jumble-sale stalls from whose stacks of clothes, single socks and the arms of

THIS PAGE Storage used as a partition or division serves a double purpose; this wall of closets divides the bathroom from the master bedroom.

sweaters or the hems of skirts protrude tantalisingly? If you could only find permanent homes for all those things and get them well and truly out of the way and beautifully stored, your abode will look a thousand times more tidy. What is more, you will, in the long run, save yourself time that would otherwise have been spent in frustrating and often fruitless searches, many of which simply add to the mass of clutter rather than eliminating it.

Finding a home for all your things is also particularly important if you share your space with other people – and most of us do at some stage of our life. Everyone, whatever their age, and no matter how personally tidy they be, brings with him his own, specific, life-related clutter and the more people there are that share a space, the more important it is to have effective and organised storage, otherwise chaos and inefficiency will ensue.

What is more, all that unstored clutter takes up space – space that can be far better used for living. The removal of clutter can open up a room in a way

ABOVE In a light-filled room, a low-built storage unit holds everything in discreet, laid-back fashion.

LEFT The china stored in this commodious antique cupboard has been arranged as much to display its beauty as to keep it close to hand.

OPPOSITE In this very masculine dressing room, as on a stage, the neatly ranged rows of polished black shoes are echoed by the graphic black-and-white curtains hanging behind them.

that you can't imagine until you try it. Ask any interior designer. One of the first things he or she thinks about is the logical organisation of the available space and the best places to stow things — from kitchen pots and pans, through home entertainment systems, to clothing and toiletries.

For those of us without access to the skills of an interior designer — or even in those homes where a designer has been, but long since gone — it is important to apply the same principles. It is really no exaggeration to say that reorganising the available space, finding the right place for all your possessions and learning the art of tidiness can literally revolutionise your home — even to the extent of removing the necessity to move. Too often a space that seems unlivable because it is too small, is simply a cramped space that needs a good de-clutter and some decent storage. As the old homily goes, 'A place for everything, and everything in its place'. Like so many sayings, this one encapsulates a genuine truth.

ABOVE A pair of freestanding, glass-fronted painted bookcases with cupboards below and pediments on top not only provide storage space but are an important part of the room's design theme.

RIGHT A passageway between the kitchen and eating area has been imaginatively transformed into a storage space, with shelves housing a collection of Kilner jars as well as china and glass.

THIS PAGE In this eccentric and pleasing living space, the wall-to-wall and floor-to-ceiling bookcase plays an essential part in maintaining a sense of order and purpose.

OPPOSITE A kitchen in a cupboard: the sliding doors open to reveal a hob, oven, sink and dishwasher, as well as cupboards to store china and glass. Above is decorative storage space for non-kitchen items such as books and pictures.

PLEASURE

OPPOSITE This wall of wood has ample shelf and cupboard space and offers a quirky way of storing the Oriental slippers hung all in a highly decorative row.

BELOW Here, built-in storage has been carefully designed to integrate with the architectural elements of this apartment, blending in with the columns and cornices of the room.

Good storage offers more, much more, than the benefits in terms of practicality and efficiency. Good storage and a well-organised home bring a sense of pleasure. Enjoy a feeling of quiet satisfaction as you contemplate a well-stocked larder with everything to hand, a stack of crisply ironed shirts readily accessible in the wardrobe, clean fluffy towels just begging to be used on a bathroom shelf, a beautiful glass-fronted armoire with its gorgeous display of sparkling clean tableware, or a writing desk with crisp, clean writing paper and pristine envelopes neatly stowed on top.

That said, every aspect of such orderly contentment is always particular to the individual – one man's pleasurable storage is another's obsessive tidiness. The neat ranging of every pair of shoes along a shoe rack could

WITH STORAGE, AS WITH SO MUCH ELSE IN LIFE, IT IS THE CASE THAT ONE MAN'S MEAT IS ANOTHER MAN'S POISON. WHAT MAY SEEM TO YOU TO BE THE PERFECT STORAGE SOLUTION MIGHT APPEAR TO SOMEONE ELSE TO BE THE HEIGHT OF OBSESSION.

ABOVE Low-level shelving reinforces the low lines of the sitting area and allows a totally unobstructed view around the room and through the windows.

OPPOSITE In the library area of an open-plan Art-Deco space, the shelving units have been designed to be at waist-height in order not to impede the sight lines through the rest of the apartment.

conceivably be seen as irritating. Having clean, folded towels out on display rather than behind closed doors where they may be stacked in less than perfect piles might seem to be a waste of time. Having one's books on the shelf and not in alphabetical author order might seem like the end of the world, while for some people keeping them tidy on the shelf in the first place might induce a sense of extreme discomfort. So, the secret in gaining most pleasure from your particular storage solutions is to seek advice from others, but then, after due consideration, to follow your own instincts; for that way – as in other areas of life – true pleasure lies.

CLEANLINESS AND SAFETY

It goes without saying that in a home where good storage systems are in place, you are likely to find a greater degree of cleanliness. And I am not just talking about clothing that is stored, dust-free behind a neat façade of closed doors or foodstuffs kept in orderly cupboards and drawers so it stays fresh and you can readily see what you have got.

No, I am also talking about the fact that in such homes, people do not have to start their cleaning with a massive tidying blitz that will enable a quick whizz with the vacuum cleaner or a hasty wipe with the household cleaner. Surfaces remain wonderfully clutter-free and cleaning time is cut in half.

And, it is a known fact that clutter that is not properly stored is potentially dangerous, especially if there are children or elderly people around. The tripped-over pile of papers, the pots and pans that fall from their unsteady stack on a shelf, the trailing computer cables, the medicines put higgledy-piggledy in a kitchen drawer. Whatever room of the house you are in, clutter can be a hazard.

THIS PAGE A wall is filled with understated cupboards with, inside, useful modules of different heights and widths.

OPPOSITE One corner of this room is a kitchen, the other a breakfast room; sleek, eye-level kitchen cupboards help define the cooking area.

Action Plan

THIS PAGE Careful planning is required to ensure that the complex storage needs of a kitchen are met and that you do not have to rummage at the back of a cupboard for that essential piece of equipment.

Nothing beats good planning in life

Nothing beats good planning in life and working out a storage action plan before you go out shopping for any type of storage solution is no exception. First you need to identify exactly what it is in your life that you want to store and whether you will be using it on a daily basis (such things obviously need to be stored close to hand), less frequently (these things can be put a bit more out of the way on high shelves or at the top of tall cupboards), or hardly ever (this is when attics and sheds come in useful). It also pays to measure the storage space you have then, hopefully, you can fill that space to best advantage with shelving, cupboards or whatever works best for you.

Let us start by taking a look at the sort of things that you, personally, need to store. Items such as kitchen utensils, cleaning materials, everyday crockery and glassware and home entertainment systems all need to be readily accessible at all times. Sports equipment, garden tools, domestic paperwork and 'best' china might be needed from time to time, while luggage, spare duvets and ski, snowboard or surfing equipment come out only a couple of times a year. Make this your starting point for successful storage every time.

TOP LEFT Most things look better when neatly stored; here, pencils in chunky glass tumblers have a grace that they would lack if they were lying at the back of a drawer.

TOP RIGHT Pots ranged on a shelf have a comforting, purposeful presence and offer the promise of good food to come.

CENTRE LEFT A collection of new glass, based on eighteenth-century designs, is stored and displayed behind the glass doors of a traditional, white-painted, built-in butler's pantry cupboard.

CENTRE RIGHT Intersperse books with small decorative objects; both are enhanced by the contrast in shape and colour.

BOTTOM LEFT On an open shelf, dried goods in glass Kilner jars of different sizes and shape have a pleasing symmetry about them.

BOTTOM RIGHT Fabric bags add a sunny air to a bathroom and are useful for storing anything from cotton wool to soap and even toothpaste and deodorant.

WHAT ARE YOU STORING?

BELOW A classic yet contemporary all-encompassing storage unit; from ground level, compartmentalised shelves hold decorative objects as well as books in both horizontal and vertical rows.

We now have so much leisure time, compared with people in the past, that a lot of what we need to store around the house is connected with the way we use that time. Many homes now have televisions, DVD players and music systems, and many have state-of-the art computer-controlled entertainment systems. Amazingly, contrary to the dire warnings of a few years ago, we still buy books, too. All these pleasant companions need a home, and that home must be pretty close to hand as well. After all, when you want to relax, you need that book or DVD now and in easy reach, not in

THIS PAGE In this bedroom, the combination of bold open shelves for the display of books and objects, combined with a low-level unit is grounded by a pair of floor-to-ceiling column lamps that give a soft light everywhere.

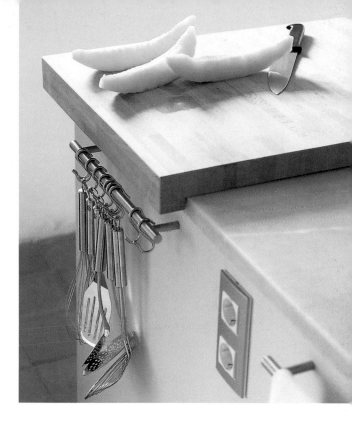

LEFT A small space is made into a super-functional bedroom and study with the area beneath the raised bed providing perfect storage space for books and work.

RIGHT This chopping board is designed to slide smoothly along the work surface to where it is needed with, below, essential work tools hung on a convenient rail.

an hour's time after an intensive search. It is daunting to find that the CD you want to listen to is in a box on the floor beneath twenty others, or that the book you want to read is on a shelf that is too high to reach.

So, when it comes to the storage of our leisure materials, as with every other aspect of storage, the first thing to decide is what you want to have on view and instantly accessible, and what you want behind doors. Obviously you need to be able to see the television screen and these are so good-looking nowadays that they are often a visual pleasure in themselves – though if your room is decorated in a traditional style, you may prefer to hide the television away. The same goes for music equipment.

What you will not want to look at – ever – is a spaghetti junction of cables and wires. For this reason, many people prefer to have a specially designed storage system, whether built-in or freestanding, for their entertainment equipment. This ensures that there is a place for everything and that everything has its place – including those well-concealed cables.

WORK STORAGE
Next comes the storage of work-related items, whether things like kitchen and food-preparation equipment or the home computer and its attendant accessories. When you are doing the cooking, the household accounts or perhaps running a business from home, it is beyond infuriating, as well as extremely inefficient, to have the tools you need stacked around the room in higgledy-piggledy fashion. This is quite apart from the utter waste of time spent searching for the right connecting cable or the whisk attachment for the blender. Later on in this book I will look at both kitchens and home offices in more detail, but here it is probably enough to say that, as with every other

storage conundrum, the first step in getting it right is to identify just what it is that you personally need to have close at hand. Different people have different priorities, so don't be cowed by what the 'experts' say. What is important is that, the homes you choose for everything – from jars of spices and wooden spoons to paper clips and staplers – work efficiently for you.

STORING CLOTHES AND LINENS

The sense of connection that we have towards the textiles we use every day – the clothes we wear, the linen we sleep on or eat from, the towels we dry ourselves with – is immense. Many people feel an almost atavistic satisfaction in having neatly ranged, clean and pressed piles of clothes and linen around them. Indeed, when moving home, however temporarily, one of the first things that many people

do, no matter how nomad-like they are in their habits, is to immediately rig up some form of shelter for their clothes – a hanging rail, some baskets, boxes or bags. The desire for order for these personal possessions and to be able to quickly find what is needed is deep-rooted.

Clean, neatly folded bed and table linen also seems to be important to our sense of wellbeing, and we like it to be stored in an equally clean and orderly manner. For hundreds of years, houses had specific storage areas for linen, from walk-in linen cupboards or linen-storage rooms to specially designed furniture such as linen presses. These combinations of cupboard and chest could hold all that was needed for both bed and bath. Today's modern equivalent might be a deep chest of drawers for folded sheets and towels, or perhaps a cheap and cheerful painted cupboard with deep shelves that can take stacks of bed and bath necessities.

OPPOSITE LEFT Hooks with a difference: these wall-mounted hook columns each have three adjustable hooks that will help keep innumerable clothes off the floor. Here, they make something of an artistic display.

OPPOSITE RIGHT The orderly man's idea of bliss: a tall storage unit of shallow shelves, each one tailored to hold a single, pristine shirt.

THIS PAGE Beneath the basin of this gleaming blue-and-white bathroom – and helping to hide the plumbing – is an open shelf for clean towels and, beneath, two rows of colourful drawers for bathroom bits and bobs that are best kept hidden from view. The concept could not be simpler nor more effective.

There are many different ways to store your things, but storage is a creative design tool as well as a practical necessity. You need it to work well, but it must also be appealing to the eye and should fit in with the style and decoration of your room.

Much of today's storage – especially the built-in or modular variety – is not an extrovert. It goes about its business quietly, blending into the background. Freestanding pieces are more likely to make a statement. You might have found a beautiful antique armoire that is perfect for storing bedding, some quirky industrial shelving that seems tailor-made for kitchen storage or a streamlined sixties sideboard that cuts a dash in the dining room.

As well as considering whether you prefer freestanding or built-in storage – and here the proportions of your room are important as well as the style – you also need to decide whether you want things on show or hidden away.

When your storage also acts as display, the arrangement of the objects is as important as the objects themselves. This type of storage might encompass collections of rare books, beautiful artefacts from around the world, family photographs or works of art, but it can equally apply to often-used items such as china and glassware or a home entertainment system.

TOP LEFT Simple and just perfect for its position in a busy hallway, an oversized, lidded woven basket can take everything that one might throw at, or in, it.

TOP RIGHT An antique or interesting piece of furniture, while being appreciated for its practical qualities, should also be given its decorative due.

CENTRE LEFT An industrial-style corner shelf unit both stores and displays a collection of drinking glasses in every conceivable colour, shape and size.

CENTRE RIGHT Tall cupboards in a dining room are screened by sliding Japanese-style paper screens that echo the design of the storage units.

BOTTOM LEFT This mobile trolley-cum-storage unit can skim across the floor to wherever it is needed, but has lockable wheels so that it will stay put when it gets there.

BOTTOM RIGHT Handles that run the full width of these shallow kitchen drawers make them extremely easy to open and close.

BUILT-IN

A wall of made-to-measure built-in storage can totally change a room. From the visual point of view it can extend and maximise the space, but it also affects the way the room works and can give new life to the way you live.

The obvious advantage of built-in storage is that it will make the best use of the space and, in a streamlined manner, will accommodate all the things that need storing. For instance, if you are having a wall of closet space installed or – even luckier – are planning a dressing room, you can have your storage built to suit the way your wardrobe works. Do you dress formally in suits or less formally in separates? Do you need storage for sportswear and sports equipment? Do you like your shirts or blouses folded or hung? What about sweaters, jackets and overcoats? How much full-length hanging space will you need, how much half-length, how many shelves, and do these all have to be full-depth for shirts and sweaters or can some be shallower, perhaps for underwear?

LEFT The joy of built-in. A curved kitchen – almost a space pod – complete with maximum storage has been cleverly constructed in a very awkward space.

RIGHT Beneath the vaulted, old brick ceiling of a converted fifteenth-century monastery, a kitchen storage unit has been designed to fit precisely into the high, arched space.

ABOVE LEFT This is an ingenious, complex storage solution; while one side of the unit houses a set of drawers, the other side (not seen) is a seating area with a banquette sofa.

ABOVE RIGHT This handsome modern built-in armoire has, behind the doors, deep shelves for large pieces of tableware and, beneath, drawers of different sizes to accommodate everything from cutlery to table linen.

Another great advantage of built-in storage is that it can be made to work perfectly with the architecture of your room and can also be used, to some measure, to correct architectural faults. It can be built around such inconveniences as pipework or internal beams, it can fit into corners and can be used to add interest to an otherwise blank wall.

Yet another advantage is that you can have it styled and finished in whatever way you choose. The options are endless, from traditional wood with mouldings to streamlined stainless steel or glass. And there is no need to stop at using only one material. You might like to combine glass and wood, leather and suede, Perspex and metal.

The disadvantages though are that built-in storage is, inevitably, expensive. It is also of course permanent, which could be considered a great disadvantage if you are thinking of moving home in the relatively near future. And as built-in storage cannot be moved from room to room it is also, of course, less adaptable than a freestanding piece.

RIGHT In this room, the entertainment equipment is housed in a tailor-made unit complete with shelves of different heights. Everything is hidden behind imposing walnut-faced floor-to-ceiling sliding doors.

BELOW Especially conceived for this particular space, a set of sleek cupboards in limed wood open with a push-touch mechanism rather than with handles that might detract from the clean lines.

THIS PAGE A built-in bed storage unit surrounds a bed with tall cupboards either side and a low-level bedhead – incorporating a horizontal light – that also acts as a bedside table.

RIGHT This smallest of kitchens, set between two living spaces, requires efficient, all-encompassing storage, as exemplified by the low-level kitchen units and the floor-to-ceiling white-faced cupboards.

STYLE, SCALE AND PROPORTION

Any piece of built-in storage is bound to be large and its size means that it is important for it to be sympathetic to the style of the room or it will simply stick out like a sore – and very big – thumb. Whether your style is modern or traditional, try and ensure that your built-in storage has a classic timelessness.

It is also important to get the scale and proportions right. The height is obviously very dependent on the dimensions of the room but it is rarely advisable to build from floor to ceiling as this can look too hemmed-in. The exception to this might be in a kitchen or bathroom where you cannot afford to waste any space. Instead it is often better to have your piece of storage furniture stop at approximately picture-rail height or slightly higher, then use concealed lighting above that to take the eye upwards to the ceiling. Or, instead of having what might be a very heavy-looking storage wall, you could have the storage begin at just above seating height so that a sofa or chairs can be placed directly beneath it. Yet another option, especially in a

from open shelves to cupboards, drawers and even slide-out work surfaces.

The size and spacing of these different elements in the storage is as important as the overall scale of the entire thing; divisions that are too large can upset the proportions of the room, small box-like divisions can give a feeling of claustrophobia.

When it comes to the cupboard doors, yet again there is a wide range of possibilities. The doors do not have to run from top to bottom if that is not what you need, nor do they have to be hinged. Sliding doors of all sizes are a useful space-saving choice. The door fronts may be of wood – moulded or plain, painted or unpainted – but equally they can be of a transparent or semi-transparent material. Colour is a powerful decorating tool so if the decorative scheme of the room calls for it, the doors could be painted in different contrasting colours or they could be faced with a textured surface such as leather or suede.

THE BUILT-IN BOOKCASE

Although not often thought of as such, one of the earliest types of built-in storage was the built-in bookcase. A feature of many old houses – sometimes as part of a dedicated library, sometimes built into the drawing room or sitting room – the built-in bookcase was as important a piece of furniture as anything else in the room, and it can still be as noteworthy and useful today. In their more traditional guise, the most versatile designs consist of shelving sitting on top of cupboards, so you get bookshelves combined with dust-proof storage and, if the cupboards are deeper than the shelving, their top surface provides a useful display surface for pictures or lamps.

If the bookcase wall is particularly long, the design can be broken up by varying the depth of the

room with a large, wide window, is to have the built-in units rising from floor to waist or window height so they do not 'fight' with the window line.

A VARIETY OF OPTIONS

Often the image of built-in storage is one of a wall of identical doors – think old-fashioned built-in wardrobes – but there is no reason why built-in nowadays should be a synonym for closed off. Depending on which room the storage system is situated in and what it is going to hold, it could combine a number of different storage options ranging

OPPOSITE Perfect living-room storage; a floor-to-ceiling wall of segmented shelving in which most things can easily be stored. Leaving the upper rows empty keeps it looking light.

THIS PAGE A wall of open storage is designed to be in tune with the eclectic decoration of the rest of the room, with books stored on either side of the central section, which is strictly for display.

cupboards, having them deeper in the central section. Moulding can be used to great effect to frame simple, wooden uprights (bold moulding is more effective than narrow) and the shelves should always be made to be adjustable. If the wood the bookcase is made from is not particularly special, you can paint it to tone with the rest of the room, but do not choose exactly the same colour as the walls; a subtle difference is much more effective. A matt finish is softer than a reflecting gloss, and a useful decorator's trick is to paint the inside of the bookshelves in a deeper tone than the surrounds.

A modern take on the built-in bookcase will almost certainly have shelves for the display of things other than books and there may well be a special niche to house the televison or home entertainment system, too.

PRACTICALITIES

If you are thinking of built-in storage, chances are that you will either be employing a skilled joiner or will use a design-and-build company. The latter are experienced in dreaming up solutions for every possible storage conundrum and they will be familiar with all the latest materials and technological advances. They will also be aware of any structural requirements and will know to ensure that – and probably also organise – any electrical work is done before the built-in is installed.

But do not leave all the planning to other people. It is really worth while drawing up a list of your own particular requirements and using that as your starting point. That way you will be sure of having the built-in storage you really need.

WITH SO MANY STORAGE SOLUTIONS TO CHOOSE FROM, STORAGE CAN BE AS DISCREET OR AS DOMINANT AS YOU WISH BUT THE BEST WILL ALWAYS FORM A SEAMLESS PART OF YOUR DECORATING SCHEME

Unexpected places

- ■ Mobile stacking storage towers will slide into narrow upright spaces.

- ■ Corner units make good use of what might otherwise be 'dead' space.

- ■ Mail-order catalogues are a surprisingly good source of unusual storage solutions.

- ■ Some mobile dress rails can be height-adjusted to fit an angled space.

For extra storage space, look beyond the obvious to the slightly more unusual – the angled area beneath the stairs or the space beneath the eaves, for instance. Look, too, at the often unnoticed alcoves formed by boxed-in pipes, as well as at the space beneath beds and windows. Built-out window seats with cupboards below serve two purposes – they offer a comfortable place to muse or read, combined with easy-to-access, deep storage. In the bedroom, consider the possibilities of a deeper-than-usual built-in headboard that offers hidden storage space accessed from above. Beneath sinks and basins are other obvious, but often ignored, spots; you can readily find store-bought shelf units that are designed to fit around plumbing and pipes.

ABOVE A narrow corridor has been re-arranged to provide an office in a cupboard with sleek sliding doors to conceal the evidence when the office is not in use.

RIGHT In a good example of original storage thinking, the space beneath this bay-window seat has been fitted with a useful deep, shallow drawer.

THIS PAGE In this large, essentially open-plan area, a system of sliding doors and freestanding room dividers makes for a functional and adaptable space, as well as offering the opportunity for a degree of privacy.

Dividing rooms

■ Colour adds definition. A unit painted in different colours on either side will help define the two spaces.

■ For each side of the divider choose decorative objects that link to the function of that side.

■ As with any storage, avoid a uniform pattern of divisions. Variety, for instance in shelf height, adds interest and a feeling of individuality.

If you have a large open-plan living area such as a converted loft apartment where you need to define the different functional areas of the room, what could be more practical than to use a room divider that doubles as a wall of storage? The secret lies in making sure that the storage-divider is deep enough and that each side is appropriate to its own space. Don't be fooled into thinking that they have to be a mirror image of one another; Janus-like, each can present a different public face. One of the most successful of this type of divider is a low-level unit, one face of which acts as a custom-made bedhead, complete with bedside shelving, built-in lighting and so on, while the other side functions either just as a plain wall or as an additional storage unit.

ABOVE Sitting well above floor level on a landing and with space above it, this dividing unit provides an airy-looking, functional alternative to a solid wall.

RIGHT An extra-deep unit combines storage space on one side – the added bonus is that this also forms the side wall for a flight of stairs – with a division from the adjoining dining area.

FREESTANDING

Freestanding storage can be as simple

or as elaborate as you like, and as economical or expensive as your budget will allow. It can be a store-bought set of bare wooden shelves, a modular designer system, a piece of reclaimed office furniture or a unique antique.

Many people on a budget start off with freestanding storage for, in theory, as their income grows, they can upgrade and perhaps use their old storage elsewhere in the home. This, of course, encapsulates a number of the advantages of freestanding storage. It can be inexpensive, it can have many different applications around the house, and when you move onwards and upwards, so can the storage.

ABOVE The simplest of freestanding pieces: an industrial shelf unit on which can be stacked everything from video tapes and books to DVDs.

RIGHT Proving that storage can be as simple as your imagination will allow: in the study area of a living room a box storage unit is exactly that – a stack of upturned old orange boxes.

THIS PAGE When you are considering freestanding storage, think laterally; many types of reclaimed items, from old kitchen ranges to filing cabinets, can be brought into use to make interesting, one-off pieces of storage.

Contemporary modular systems, shelving units and sideboards – which have recently made a comeback – are much beloved of modern furniture designers and offer some state-of-the-art storage solutions for living and dining rooms, bedrooms and the home office. They are also available in every manner of finish and material such as wood, metal, plastic and glass or in combinations of the above.

You might also spare a thought for well-designed nineteenth and early twentieth-century pieces of furniture such as the cupboard, the wardrobe, the chest of drawers and its more refined cousins, the tallboy and the lowboy. You can buy worthwhile pieces that still serve their purpose well and can be passed onto future generations to solve their storage problems.

One of the most adaptable of pieces since it was first thought of, probably in the 1700s, is the painted continental armoire, which is once again so popular that modern versions are now readily available. The originals were often a combination of a cupboard on top of a set of drawers. The doors of the cupboard were either solid wood or glazed while in some, the doors were filled with wire mesh or ruched fabric. In other versions there might be open shelves above and small drawers and/or a cupboard below, rather like a dresser. This adaptability explains the armoire's new popularity; its latest

ABOVE An imposing twentieth-century Danish cabinet stands proud and aloof in this severely perfect dining room.

LEFT A low-level, freestanding wooden unit makes a bold composition with the striking painting in this room, especially when the two are anchored by a pair of table lamps.

OPPOSITE ABOVE This set of wooden storage modules, combined in such a way as to offer a variety of levels, gives a textural contrast with the brick wall.

OPPOSITE BELOW A pair of tall, dark-wood cabinets are used not only to store dining-room essentials, but also to make a dramatic frame around the imposing door of this London dining room.

GOOD STORAGE
SOLUTIONS ARE ALWAYS
AS IMPORTANT TO THE
OVERALL DESIGN OF THE
ROOM AS EVERY OTHER
PIECE OF FURNITURE TO
BE FOUND THEREIN

incarnation is as a home office where it can hold all your necessities –
computer, printer and stationery.

Freestanding bookcases are an obvious storage possibility but they do not
have to serve just to house books. They can be used as effectively as their
built-in counterparts for televisions and music systems. And if you do want to
have a bookcase made, you could go for a triangular or pyramidal shape and
perhaps have a pair. One either side a door or window gives an added
architectural and decorative element to the room.

RECLAIM AND RECONFIGURE

Some of today's most innovative storage solutions come in the form of
reclaimed pieces that are given a new lease of life in the modern home, and
sometimes are used for a totally different purpose from that for which they
were originally designed. The simplest examples are old – but not valuable –
cupboards or wardrobes from a junk shop. The insertion of shelves into a
sturdy but ugly dark wood wardrobe, followed by a coat of paint and some

ABOVE A family heirloom,
this armoire is used to
store everything from linen
to clothes to crockery.

ABOVE LEFT Shelves
above an old painted
bathroom cupboard
provide a platform for an
exuberant display of
treasured objects.

RIGHT An antique painted
desk is about as pretty a
piece of storage as you
could find. Cherished for
its decorative value, it is
also functional, keeping
papers and writing
materials in good order.

new handles can give you a handsome, original and extremely useful piece of freestanding storage that does not have to be used only in the bedroom.

Or you might come across an old school tuck box or metal school trunk, which can be used to house toys, books or CDs and DVDs, or an old wooden shop counter or plan chest which can be very effective as kitchen or home-office storage.

Then there is storage that is inspired by the early loft conversions of the 1960s where reclaimed industrial storage gave just the right utilitarian look. Extremely hard-working, adaptable and immensely flexible, reclaimed industrial units are easy to clean up and can be painted if you wish. Industrial metal shelving and metal cupboards are examples of what you can find if you know where to look (see Suppliers, page 136–141) and, since much of it is modular, it can be added to or moved around to create new storage configurations. Old pieces such as these give individuality to a room that a new piece can never offer.

LEFT With a nod to the twentieth century, this arrangement shows that freestanding storage can be enormously chic as well as unexpected.

RIGHT In a contemporary, originally styled room, a clever freestanding low shelving unit hides its stored contents behind semi-opaque doors which add extra interest to the general décor.

MOBILE STORAGE

The most freestanding of all storage is the mobile sort that can be moved to wherever is most convenient. Over the last few years, it has enjoyed great popularity, particularly in the kitchen where it sometimes takes the shape of a big butcher's block on wheels, sometimes with space to hang a towel, drawers for kitchen knives, hanging vegetable baskets and a lower shelf to store crockery or condiments. In the living room, a mobile storage unit might house your television and DVD player, with shelves or drawers for DVDs and videos, while your home office could consist of a wheeled unit for computer, files and other office necessities. This can be quickly wheeled out of sight – an eminently practical idea, particularly if your home office is in the living room or if you live in a studio flat.

Mobile storage is found in the bedroom, too. Once we only had ugly hanging rails on wheels, which look fine if your home is an industrial-style loft and all you have to store are clothes on hangers. Now you can find sectioned mesh hanging storage bags to suspend from the rail to accommodate your sweaters and shoes, or you might choose one of the more sophisticated wheeled units that incorporate a shelf in addition to a hanging rail. These often have a heavy canvas cover to keep your clothes dust-free.

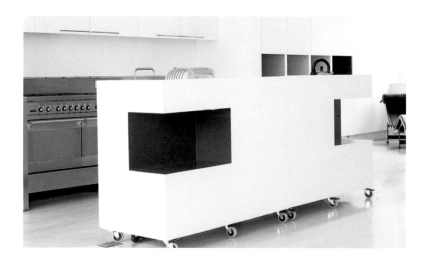

ABOVE In a very small bedroom, a flexible storage unit on wheels that can be easily moved – or removed – is a clever solution.

LEFT Incorporated into this oversized island unit is not only a ceramic hob, but also a comprehensive range of low-level storage units on castors that can be moved to where they will be of most use.

OPPOSITE This very contemporary mobile island unit, on locking wheels, consists of two connecting pieces. It can be used as part of the kitchen area, or moved back out of the way when meals take place.

OPEN SHELVING

BELOW LEFT Colour is an ever-useful tool. Here, suspended from the ceiling, red-lacquered shelving appears to free-float against the window, highlighting the display of white crockery.

BELOW RIGHT Open-fronted units take up just the right amount of wall space. The effect is almost sculptural.

OPPOSITE When does open shelving become a piece of furniture? Perhaps here, through the simple device of painting the wall behind in a bright contrasting colour.

Open shelving may well be the simplest form of storage, but it is also – potentially – one of the most striking and most effective. It can range from the basic – untreated, easy-to-erect wooden shelves bought in a DIY store – to the sophisticated and costly, which might be a carefully considered and specially designed storage system that fulfils every possible storage need from housing a sound system or a library to displaying an art collection.

You can choose from a huge range of shelving materials of which wood – which comes in many types and colours – is only one. Then there are MDF and metal, which, like wood, can be painted, and there are also stone and glass. The important thing is to consider what surface and material will work best with the other furniture in your room.

IN THE KITCHEN, OPEN
SHELVING CAN SOLVE MANY
STORAGE PROBLEMS,
ESPECIALLY THAT OF HOW
TO STORE OFTEN-USED
EQUIPMENT AND SUPPPLIES

At its simplest, you might just want some open
shelving to cope with a small storage problem – an
excess of books being the most common. If a location
for your shelves does not immediately spring to mind,
go round your living space looking for unexpected
corners and niches where the odd shelf might be
employed. For example, one or two shelves hung in the
often dead space above a door is a useful place for books
that you want but don't need on a daily basis. The space
between a kitchen counter and the cabinets above
might be home to a shallow set of shelves holding small
bottles and jars, or glassware, all within easy reach.

LEFT In a former brick factory, freestanding stainless-steel units and wall-mounted shelves for the kitchen equipment, look appropriately rugged and in keeping with the industrial space.

RIGHT Shelves that look as if they float are in fact attached by rods hidden within the kitchen wall. They take up minimal space and continue the line of the narrow, below-counter shelving.

Also in the kitchen, deep open shelving high on the wall is a good place to keep those larger pieces of equipment that you want to have around but do not use all the time – the fish kettle, the large stockpot or the casserole dishes. Having your utensils on show gives an impression of a kitchen that is well used and comforting, although the equipment might get a little dirtier than when it is kept behind closed doors.

Open shelving high on the wall works well in a child's room, too. Here you could store toys that have been grown out of but are still loved. Decorative in their own right, they give a child a sense of security.

With thorough planning, open shelving can make a statement in any room, but for it to be successful, it is essential that the design and dimensions form part of your overall decorative scheme. Not only should the shelving be in keeping with the room's style, but proportion and scale must be taken into account. For instance, a run of open shelving should make best use of the entire wall space. Nothing is less effective than a set of shelves marooned in a sea of wall to which it seems to bear no relation. Nor should you be afraid of using chunky shelving if space allows. It can be far more effective than its half-hearted lightweight cousin.

REVEAL OR CONCEAL

What to display, and what not to display? That is the question. The answer depends to some extent on the room. You are more likely to want to display your possessions in one of the rooms that other people see, but it can give you great pleasure to have your clothes or a collection of your favourite things beautifully displayed in the bedroom or to have things that relate to a particular hobby – certain tools and paintbrushes or knitting wools and embroidery threads can look good – out on show in your hobby room. Or you might choose to combine the functional with the decorative by, for instance, having a display of copper pans or of china and glassware in the kitchen. It may be that only you and your family sees it, but it can make a kitchen look warm and homely and you will enjoy cooking all the more.

The display of objects that form part of a collection is another matter and you may well want to have these on more public show. Grouped cleverly – for, as any decorator will tell you, everything looks better arranged as a group rather than having one piece here and another there – and with wit, your collection will straight away gain in visual importance. You might try arranging it on a simple shelf or shelves, on shelves divided into sections to make individual cubbyholes or in wall-hung open-fronted boxes.

LEFT The traditional dresser makes the perfect backdrop for the display and safe storage of a collection of antique transferware, particularly when – as here – the shelves have been painted to harmonise. Cupboards below keep other items dust-free.

RIGHT A built-in cabinet spans part of a wall but is not flush with it; around it has been built shelving for books and ornaments. The contrast of open and closed storage is pleasingly balanced.

LEFT Missing only the kitchen sink, the arrangement and variety of pieces on and in this fine Welsh dresser is an object lesson in how to combine sensible storage with eye-catching display.

RIGHT Instant display: a collection of pretty, vintage beaded handbags hanging from small cup hooks are stored but also displayed in all their finery.

BELOW RIGHT In an open-plan loft, these simple shelves displaying a varied and eclectic collection of glass, define and mark out the dining area.

How you display the individual items is a question of achieving a balance between their shape and size and the storage they sit in. Large objects – art works or sculptural pieces, perhaps – look best in sectioned, cubbyhole-type storage with one piece per section. Each object then has room to breathe, as it were. Smaller objects look better tightly grouped along a short shelf or stack of such shelves, or with groups of objects separated by uprights.

Time-honoured ways of breaking up the monotony of a book collection are to leave some space between groups of books and/or intersperse the books with other items – the occasional picture, figurine, piece of china or pottery. Just bear in mind the scale; it is no use putting a tiny porcelain figurine alongside a row of chunky reference books.

MATERIAL MATTERS

Another point to consider is what the shelving or display boxes are to be made of. Here it is a question of balancing the mass of the item or items to be

LEFT Traditional-style bookshelves are painted a soft green to contrast with the white-jacketed books.

FAR LEFT A collection of model trucks and cars is displayed with simple glassware, which highlights the intricacy of the models.

BELOW LEFT Successful storage has as much to do with joinery as with presentation: a fine collection of creamy china jugs distracts the eye from the radiator panel below.

RIGHT Beneath framed children's dress patterns in a fashion designer's studio, a system of small boxes provides efficient storage for everything from buttons to sketches.

displayed with that of the shelving. The rule usually is to combine heavy items with heavy shelving and more insubstantial pieces with lighter-looking shelving, but sometimes you can have a very successful contrast. A collection of fragile glass, for instance, will look best arranged on glass shelves either on their own on a wall or within a larger storage unit where, if lit from underneath, the pieces take on an almost ethereal quality. Another effective solution is to display the collection on glass shelves in front of a window. Here, once again, the glass will appear to float in mid-air. Similarly, a display of dark wood tribal art will look eye-catching framed by chunky white shelves and uprights or it could look equally spectacular on heavy glass shelving. What will not work, though, is combining the

heavy dark wood pieces with lightweight glass shelves. They will not only appear uncomfortable, but will probably be unsafe, too.

Think also about the style and period of your room when choosing your style of display. If you have a traditional room, it is more usual to choose a piece of display furniture to match, but if you have a good eye, a contrast can be very eye-catching — antique china or glass in a cutting-edge contemporary storage unit or pieces of modern designer pottery in a period cabinet.

Remember, too, that your display does not have to be static. Take a tip from the art galleries and change things around once in a while so your eye does not get stale. A changing display will ask the viewer to re-assess and re-evaluate the objects in it.

THIS PAGE Bright pink-painted doors are filled with acid-etched glass which adds a gentle glow to the light inside the cupboard as well as concealing the contents stored within.

Lighting

- Lighting associated with display-type storage should be discreet rather than immediately noticeable.

- Dimmers are an inexpensive way of changing the emphasis of lighting behind, above or below shelves.

- Install any lighting at the same time as you are building in storage to avoid an ugly tangle of wires and visible switches.

Being able to see what you've got stored is crucial to the success of any storage, whether it is used for displaying objects or hiding them away. Lighting in display-type storage units is an important element of the total effect. Directional spot-lighting highlights a specific item or items; concealed uplights or wall washers will backlight the whole collection.

Cupboards become infinitely more accessible if they have an interior light that comes on when the door is opened. Interior lighting is also very effective in a cupboard with glazed or semi-opaque glass doors. In a glazed cupboard, it works much like lighting on open shelves; in a cupboard with semi-opaque doors, the lighting gives a diffused effect which is a decorative feature in itself.

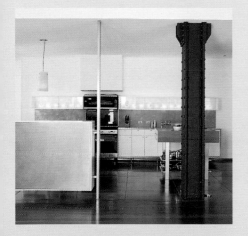

ABOVE A sophisticated, soft touch in an otherwise hard-edged kitchen is the back-lit glass cabinet that runs the length of the work surface; wine glasses stored there become decorative objects.

RIGHT Beautifully made deep shelves are subtly lit, giving the right atmosphere to this collection of museum-quality objects.

What Goes Where?

THIS PAGE A large living area in a loft space has the simplest of storage units combining open shelves and cupboards. Used mostly for display, the units also conceal more practical objects.

You may live in one room, you may live in several but wherever and however you live, what gets stored in which room is one of the most important things to get right. It really is worth spending as much time planning your storage as you do working out your lighting, flooring and colour schemes. The cleverest storage planning involves taking your entire living space into account and breaking it down room by room or area by area, thinking carefully about the function and use of each. Certain rooms have obvious functions — a kitchen must accommodate the things you need for preparing food, the living room will probably be home to your television, DVD player and music system, your bedroom will be where you store your clothes, and the dining room, if you have one, will be the most convenient place to have your china, glassware, tablecloths, placemats and napkins. But it is not always quite as easy as that. So many rooms today have a multi-functional role — one room might double up as an office, spare room and mini-gym, another might be used for cooking, eating and homework or, in a studio apartment, your living area might also be where you cook, eat and sleep. But, for successful storage, what is important is to identify and hold clearly in your mind, before you start, just what activities take place where.

TOP LEFT A clean and neat arrangement of open storage in this airy bedroom is provided by shelves anchored by metal uprights. They hold a varied collection of books, objects and works of art.

TOP RIGHT This well-designed bedside table is simplicity itself — nothing more than a wooden drawer on a curved steel wall support.

CENTRE LEFT A painted armoire with wire mesh doors above and cupboards below holds everything that is needed, and more, in this rustic dining room.

CENTRE RIGHT In a small room, one wall of which is taken up by a window, neat, unobtrusive white-painted shelves are long enough to hold all the necessities.

BOTTOM LEFT Classically styled bookshelves above base cupboards fit discreetly into alcoves either side of the fireplace in this period house.

BOTTOM RIGHT This island unit and breakfast bar combination has deep storage cupboards facing the kitchen area and an open section for display on the other side.

OPPOSITE This lofty
warehouse space has an
entire storage wall devoted
to audio-visual enjoyment.

BELOW LEFT In a storage
unit combining shelving
and deep drawers, the
higher shelves are reached
by a ladder on castors.

BELOW RIGHT A low-level
storage unit follows
exactly the line of the
high-level windows above,
unifying and consolidating
the space.

LIVING ROOMS

Today's living rooms have to work hard. Far from being rooms we enjoyed only on occasion, as happened in the past, today's living rooms live up to their name and beyond. They are used by many different people and age groups and many different activities take place there, from reading, listening to music and watching television, to doing homework or keeping our home administration in order. They may also have to function as a communal eating area for family meals and as a place to entertain friends. And, quite often, all these activities have to take place, sometimes simultaneously, in a relatively small space. What all this requires, therefore, is clever living-room storage. So how best to achieve it?

THIS PAGE In a large apartment, an ingenious and stylish storage unit combines a set of steps leading to the bedroom beyond with clever low-level shelving.

First you need to evaluate the room and try and see it as a newcomer might, with a fresh and possibly critical eye. Note what existing storage solutions you have and decide if they are adequate. If they are not, do they comprise, in principle, the right sort of storage? Do you simply need more of the same, variations on a theme or something completely different?

To help you decide, make a list of all the activities that take place in the room, both regularly and less frequently, then think of what items and equipment, both large and small, those activities require. Now you must consider what you want on view and what hidden away (see pages 66–71). Some people, for example, like to have their television and home entertainment equipment on permanent view or to have a welcoming display of drinks and glasses or a stack of magazines ready to hand. Others prefer a minimal approach which involves having it all behind closed doors.

MIX-AND-MATCH STORAGE

In order to cater for the many different functions of the room and for the variety of objects you will be wanting to store, it is most likely that you will need more than one type of storage. Some will be of the large-to-medium-sized permanent type – open shelving or drawers, or cupboards with either hide-away or see-through fronts – while other storage needs will be met by the small pick-up-and-go variety – baskets and boxes or such like. I know of one magnificent, multi-purpose living-room bookcase that runs the length of a large wall with open shelves above and cupboards below. An entire library is stored on the shelves while the cupboards conceal a wine store, a printer and stationery, DVDs and videos, a collection of vinyl records and a selection of children's toys. This bookcase is, in fact, no less than a life in a single cupboard.

At the other end of the size spectrum, do not underestimate the usefulness of all those clever, small pieces of multi-functional furniture. Many people nowadays, for instance, instead of coffee tables, have upholstered hinged and lidded ottomans. These are ideal places to store everything from games to DVDs, books and magazines. And instead of a side table at the end of a sofa, try lacquered tea chests, wicker or bamboo hampers, old cabin trunks or even metal tuck boxes. They are both decorative and practical, though you will no doubt end up putting things on top as you would a side table, so make sure you use them to store less-used items.

Any or all of these storage solutions might be just what you require. The trick is to have a flexible approach and use whatever solutions meet your needs.

ABOVE LEFT An eye-catching sofa is set off by a pleasingly clever set of bookshelves designed to sit either side of and above windows screened by a stainless-steel mesh panel.

LEFT In this Paris apartment, bookcases have been built out to meet the chimney breast and now form a pleasing, surround to the two doors that lead from the room.

RIGHT An imposing, neo-classical bookcase, designed in the 1940s by André Arbus, houses a collection of books as well as other treasures, all stored together in a calculated jumble.

LEFT This magnificent
custom-built cabinet, made
from maple with cherry-
wood inlay, is home to an
entire leisure centre
including a television, DVD
and video equipment.

STORAGE THAT SUITS THE ROOM

It is easy to forget, when you are leafing through a well-
produced glossy brochure or walking through an
attractive furniture showroom, that storage units are
not just functional necessities to be chosen on their
practical merits. They must also, especially in the case of
the living room, be carefully considered in conjunction
with the style and size of the room, for the living room
is, for better or worse, the room on which your taste
and even your way of life are judged by others. Any
storage solution should form an intrinsic part of the
décor, working with and complementing the other
pieces of furniture and balancing them out rather than
overpowering them. So, for example, a set of shelves on
one side of a room will look best when it is balanced on
the other side by a piece of furniture of equal 'weight'
and bulk. You need to find that sense of inner harmony.

You must also consider the size of your living room.
A large room may need to be broken up, and for this
you could use storage that doubles as a room divider
(see pages 50–51). Most designers agree on the
advisability of breaking up large spaces. The idea of a
vast living room like an arena, bounded only by four
walls, holds no appeal. Divisions not only add scale but
also a sense of warmth and, importantly, of domestic
life. Room-dividing storage fits the bill with ease.

If your living room is small, you might naturally
tend to choose small pieces of furniture – and storage
solutions are, really, just another type of furniture. The

result can be fussy though, so instead, take a tip from interior designers; large-scaled pieces of furniture can make a small room look much bigger. So be bold and think about covering an entire wall with storage. Not only will it provide a home for everything that is necessary for the functions of your small living room, but it will magically leave the rest of the room looking clutter-free and feeling spacious.

STYLES AND MATERIALS

Luckily there are enough differing styles of storage to appeal to everyone's taste. You may veer towards the contemporary, the semi-industrial, the classical, or the traditional. Whichever it is, you will find a look for your storage that attracts you. You may even, as with other

WHEN CONSIDERING STORAGE FOR AN INFORMAL YET TRADITIONAL LIVING ROOM, IT IS MORE SUCCESSFUL TO USE PRETTY, EVERYDAY PIECES OF FURNITURE RATHER THAN PURPOSE-BUILT UNITS

LEFT A room where storage comes in all shapes and forms as long as it is in the shape of a chest; piled high by the sofa, these oriental chests are decorative but also play a functional role.

BELOW A carved Indian cupboard with its many drawers is not only a commodious storage piece but also, as a fine piece of furniture, forms the focal point of the room. More storage space is provided beneath the coffee table.

OPPOSITE BELOW LEFT Where occasional storage is concerned, look for furniture that pays its way; here a painted coffee table has a deep lower shelf on which all the books and magazines that accumulate in a room can be neatly stored.

OPPOSITE BELOW RIGHT In a small country sitting room, painted furniture gives a calm atmosphere, and the low painted storage cupboard and wall cupboard above fit in well with the rest of the room.

elements in the home, mix and match periods and styles, but to get this right, you need to have a good eye and a courageous instinct.

Today there are as many types of materials as there are styles of storage, and they come in all price ranges. At the lower end of the scale, think MDF or wood veneer. Then there are laminate, glass, metal or Perspex – or clever combinations of these.

But the material that often seems to work best in most living areas is wood. The range of tones and colours and the depth, warmth and texture of wood in all its variety, means that you can always find a wood that will work with the other elements in the room. You can choose from pale finishes such as ash or beech, the distinctively grained oak or maple, or a dark, rich wood such as iroko or merbau. And suffice it to say that designers love to work with wood – witness the most innovative and imaginative storage systems available on the market today.

LEFT An open, airy interior filled with modern art offers the opportunity of displaying a large flat television screen as if it were another piece of art.

RIGHT The problem here was how to make a relaxed viewing area in what is essentially an open-plan living space. The solution, with the help of clever storage, was to create a book-filled den within the open-plan area. The unit housing the books and television screen, together with the comfortable chair and footstool, combine to create an atmosphere of comfort and ease.

HOME ENTERTAINMENT

Twenty-first-century home entertainment systems often take pride of place in our living rooms but it is not always easy to fit them into a decorative scheme. Happily, the two elements can be harmoniously intertwined and in the best of schemes there is an almost symbiotic relationship between them.

Although the flat-screen television is not yet completely ubiquitous, its falling cost means that it is bound to become a more common feature of our homes. From the point of view of housing and display, this can only be a good thing, as flat and slim is always easier to integrate than fat and bulbous.

A flat screen can be incorporated with hardly any loss of aesthetic appeal in almost any storage system. What you also have to factor in, though, is the concealment of the cables, plugs and other essential paraphernalia. If you are building a storage system from scratch you can, of course, take this into account in the design. You might, for example, include a drawer or niche to house the many separate and often confusing controls. Nothing is worse than a screen that is too high or low for comfortable viewing, or one that is precariously perched on a slightly too shallow ledge or shelf, so bear this in mind at the planning stage as well.

KITCHENS

BELOW In this gleaming white kitchen, push-touch doors conceal most things, including the refrigerator, but a salvaged shelf unit in glass and chrome stores a few essential cooking items where they will be needed most.

BELOW RIGHT A neat countertop hob set in a long, narrow peninsular work surface has a range of shallow drawers beneath for essential cooking utensils.

More than any other room, the kitchen is synonymous with clever storage and designers of kitchen furniture are particularly inventive. In my experience, in any household there will be more thought, more conversation, more research done about and into kitchen storage than about almost all the other storage in the home. And rightly so for, if you don't get culinary storage right, the chaos that ensues will, like Topsy, just grow and grow. That is because there are many different things that need storing in the kitchen and a working kitchen is busy, hence the need for there to be a place for everything and everything in its place.

Although the kitchen has its own unique storage problems, the solutions are, overall, the same as those generally associated with all domestic storage. You have to start by making some decisions: what items must be on hand for daily use? What is needed once or twice a month? What sort of storage makes

THIS PAGE Open shelves at one end of an island unit conveniently hold china and glass for use at the eating bar that forms one side of the unit.

THIS PAGE There is a sense of order and symmetry in the way that the crockery and glasses have been stored on deep open shelves in this simple, satisfying country kitchen.

RIGHT An example of interesting contrast; the doors of the lower cabinets are in a dark, matt finish, while those of the wall cupboards have a high-shine, mirrored surface.

OPPOSITE Dark wood-fronted storage units with a decorative grain make a strong contrast to the reflective surface of the big, American-style fridge/freezer.

ergonomic sense, for example are drawers better than cupboards? And, of course, what about a larder or pantry? From saucepans to spoons, butter to beans, food processors to flour, it is essential that you can lay your hands on ingredients and equipment without scrabbling around and lifting up heavy things to get at something hidden at the back.

STYLE DECISIONS

Old illustrations of bygone country kitchens show how important an orderly kitchen has always been – think rows of mirror-shine copper pans hung on walls, sideboards stacked with pewter and wooden dishes, deep kitchen hearths that are home to fat-bellied iron pots hung on trivets, equipment hooked onto racks hanging low over sturdy kitchen tables.

This look still has its appeal today and can be emulated in a twenty-first-century manner. With the exception of electrical kitchen appliances, kitchen equipment and even utensils have changed remarkably little over the last few hundred years, and an 'unfitted' kitchen furnished with solid wood pieces rather than with modern tailored units can still be enormously practical today. Such a kitchen might include a dresser with shelves and cupboards for china and glassware, a wooden table with drawers for cutlery and perhaps with a shelf beneath for pots and pans at ankle level, a cupboard for foodstuffs, further freestanding open shelves and a deep ceramic sink and wooden draining board set on top of a waist-high cupboard.

At the other extreme of the design scale, an enormous amount of thought and imagination has been put into contemporary, state-of-the-art kitchens. They have no end of ingenious solutions – and for problems you hadn't even thought of. Here a cupboard door is rarely just a door. Hanging from the inside you

might find racks or lipped shallow shelves to hold small bottles and jars. And the door may be attached to swing-out shelves for storing awkwardly shaped food packages or kitchen equipment. Nor is a drawer necessarily just a drawer (see pages 100–101). It can house pots and pans or it can be transformed into a pull-out shelf with sections for cutlery or kitchen knives. Often characterised by sleek, easy-clean surfaces made of laminate, wood, stone, glass and metal, ultra-modern kitchens are places where storage really works hard. And no wonder, for the look is uncluttered and minimal. Nothing is out of place, just as in a laboratory.

If this is far too sterile for your taste, you might prefer a kitchen that is inspired by both worlds – the traditional and the contemporary – and one that combines some of the more ingenious trendsetting interior storage solutions with cabinets and shelves that look less stark and clinical and that allow more of your kitchen stuff to be on show.

Which brings us to the question of what to reveal and what to conceal (see pages 66–71). This debate is particularly pertinent in the kitchen, where cooking on a hob will, by definition, make things dirtier than in other rooms, no matter how good the extractor fan

FAR LEFT In a kitchen that is a mix of contemporary and retro, stainless-steel shelves set beneath the worktop with white cupboards either side complement the stainless-steel cupboard by the door.

LEFT This kitchen has simply designed open shelving for china and glass that cleverly echoes the ceiling beams above.

LEFT BELOW Every nook and cranny in this sloping-walled kitchen has been utilised to provide shelving for the collection of white- and cream-glazed faïence.

RIGHT An unusual and striking way of storing glasses; short pegs of wood are attached in pairs to the ceiling beams and the foot of a glass slots between each pair.

you have installed. If you are thinking of going down the traditional kitchen route, where you can enjoy the comforting homeliness of seeing the ingredients and tools of your kitchen trade around you, this is an important point to consider. There is no escaping the fact that they will get grubby and greasy. Or there is another style option and that is to store things in open-fronted cupboards and to protect them not with doors but with simple curtains hung on metal rails or wires. Or you may prefer to have everything put away out of sight, with just a pristine work surface visible. This is obviously the cleanest option of all. The choice is yours.

WHAT GOES WHERE

Everyone has their own particular, way of working in the kitchen so you need to see how exactly you, personally, use the space. It is easy, for example, to say that pots and pans should be kept near the cooking area, but does that mean next to the hob or next to the oven, and is there a surface on which they can be placed when hot? And should these often quite heavy objects be kept in drawers or cupboards? I favour drawers as, providing they open and close smoothly, they are easier on the back. Equally, if you regularly use a food processor, you will want it readily accessible on the

kind of storage by the hob for all those small jars and bottles of seasoning and spices that are used by every cook. Narrow shelves – bottle depth – set close to the cooking area are an untold boon.

Last but not least, there is the question of whether or not to have a pantry or larder. Since kitchens were first built, this type of cupboard has been an integral part of the cooking complex. Even after fridges were first introduced, new kitchens – even relatively small ones – were built with a pantry. And what storage heaven it was, with every tin, bottle and package neatly ranged on wooden shelves, a deep stone or marble shelf to keep cheese and cooked dishes, and space below for sacks and bags of pulses and dry goods. A meat safe hung on the wall and the whole larder was ventilated through a mesh-covered window. Although few homes can spare the space for a walk-in pantry today, many designers are once more making pantry cupboards that have all the above and also incorporate slot-in baskets for airy storage of vegetables.

work surface, while everyday crockery and cutlery should be stored near the sink and dishwasher.

And then there are all the things that are not so often used – the industrial-sized roasting pan for the turkey, the oversized earthenware dish for the family-and-friends lasagne, the fish kettle, the jam pan and the ice-cream maker. All these can be stored in more out-of-the-way places at the back of a deep cupboard or on a high shelf, reached by a ladder if need be.

Many kitchens these days are designed around an island unit which might contain the hob and/or oven or the sink. These units give you scope for appropriate storage – deep drawers for pots and pans, a cupboard for cleaning materials, shallow drawers for cutlery. Personally, I am amazed by how few kitchens have any

THIS PAGE Glass-fronted cupboards offer the perfect combination of displaying a lovely collection of china and glass while keeping it clean and dust-free.

OPPOSITE ABOVE This narrow kitchen boasts a pair of all-encompassing shelving units made from metal. Widely available and totally adjustable, they can hold everything needed in the well-equipped kitchen.

OPPOSITE BELOW New, but seemingly old, these below-worktop kitchen storage units are designed to work well with the consciously old-fashioned design of this kitchen.

Kitchen drawers

- Silver-plated cutlery is best stored in drawers lined in baize or felt to avoid scratching the metal.

- Narrow spaces can be fitted with small drawers to hold napkins, cloths, tea towels and plastic storage bags.

- Ensure that the bottoms of drawers used to store food items have a wipe-down surface so any spills or drips can easily be cleaned off. Adhesive plastic for this purpose is readily available.

The kitchen drawer has many roles; it can be the place to store everything from tins and jars, to pots, pans and roasting trays as well as tools and utensils. Rather than letting your kitchen equipment rattle around like a pile of twigs, install some user-friendly drawer divisions. The simplest of these are widely available plastic cutlery trays that just slip into a drawer, or wooden cutlery and utensil trays that can adjust to fit different-sized drawers. Today's kitchen manufacturers offer wide spring-loaded drawers that shut with the slightest touch of the hand. The shallow drawers can hold pots and pans without the need for them to be stacked, while the deep ones can be fitted with plate racks. If you are fortunate enough to have a made-to-measure kitchen, you can have bagatelle-like pegs to sub-divide drawers or solid divisions carefully calculated to accommodate your particular collection of equipment.

ABOVE LEFT A specially designed knife drawer where every knife has its place.

ABOVE RIGHT For ease of access, many people prefer to keep their kitchen pots and pans in drawers rather than having them rattling around in a cupboard.

BELOW LEFT Innovative dishwasher drawers are a new way of storing and washing crockery and cutlery.

LEFT Good silver cutlery should always be kept in a felt-lined drawer to prevent scratching; a counsel of perfection is to lay a matching soft cloth on top.

RIGHT Simple in concept and totally practical, the angled base of this knife drawer means that the cutting edge of each knife is protected from damage.

SOMEWHERE TO EAT

Many homes nowadays are so compact that there is no dedicated dining room but instead the kitchen incorporates an eating area. When space is truly limited, there won't be room for extra storage units and you will have to stow your dining things in the kitchen cupboards and on the kitchen shelves, so you may need to severely limit the amount you have to what is absolutely essential.

If there is enough space to site the eating area a small distance from the working area, you can make it more relaxed, hospitable and diner-friendly. You might also have room to include some dining-specific storage such as a freestanding cupboard or sideboard. This can be where you store table linens, cutlery, china and, importantly, serving dishes, since these occupy a lot of space that you don't want taken up in the cooking area. Such a cupboard can also be where you store the decorative side of dining – the candlesticks, pretty bowls and small vases that you use as table decoration. All you need to do is ensure that the piece of furniture

WHEN THE KITCHEN IS USED NOT ONLY FOR COOKING BUT ALSO FOR EATING, A HOME MUST BE FOUND FOR THE CHINA AND GLASS SO THEY ARE CLOSE AT HAND AND EASILY ACCESSIBLE

ABOVE The deep mantel shelf above the range in this kitchen is a clever answer to the problem of how to store pieces of different shapes and sizes.

FAR LEFT When storage is display and vice versa; this fine set of copper pans is stored on top of the row of eye-level cupboards and cooker hood.

LEFT This tailor-made wine rack is immensely practical as well as adding a decorative feature to a modern kitchen.

RIGHT An antique painted cupboard is a traditional form of kitchen storage, holding everything from china to glassware and even bulkier items.

you choose is in harmony with the rest of the kitchen, so if the kitchen is rather classic in style, avoid having a very contemporary sideboard as the two will fight with each other. However, you may well be able to get away with a dramatic one-off cupboard – antique or classic – in a modern kitchen.

If you are lucky enough to have a separate dining room, you have more flexibility when it comes to choosing a style. No longer do you have to ensure that the dining area sits well with the kitchen. You probably will also have more room to make a bold storage statement, such as a large display of china or glass, either on open shelves or behind glass doors. Or, if you like them, you might opt for one of those terrific retro-style sideboards that are so very now.

ABOVE This entire room is decorated around the theme and colours of the china pieces that are displayed in the painted wooden dresser.

LEFT This dresser, or hutch, is actually a hybrid piece made from a base bought in a sale with shelves built above it; it suits its purpose perfectly.

OPPOSITE In this country dining room, an armoire, smaller than the norm, sits neatly behind the door. In traditional style, the shelves are decorated with a scalloped edging.

THIS PAGE A sleekly modern dining room includes a contemporary take on the traditional sideboard. The silver tea service on top provides a witty reference to traditional tea-times.

OPPOSITE This is a dining area with everything designed to fit into a 1950s decorative scheme – for instance, the mustard-coloured sliding doors of the freestanding cabinet echo the style of the Fornasetti chairs.

THIS PAGE A luxurious set of glass-fronted cupboards that reach ceiling height hold all the household china and glass within easy reach yet out of harm's way. The contents can be seen at a glance.

China and glass

- Store glasses upright – the rim is the weakest part and can easily chip on a shelf.

- Stack hand-painted or gilded plates with a napkin between each one to avoid damage.

- Do not hang old cups on hooks; the handle is the weakest part.

- Do not push stoppers too far into glass decanters or they will get stuck.

Although you could, if you wished, keep your china and glass stored in a cupboard, many of us prefer to have it on display to derive maximum pleasure from it. Unless you don't mind regular cleaning, it is usually preferable to keep it behind glass doors. There are attractive glass-fronted shelf units and cabinets on the market to suit all tastes. When you are arranging your things, treat them as you would any other arrangement. Try groupings that roughly match in volume and weight, which usually means not mixing the glass in with the china, or perhaps go for a more higgledy-piggledy country-house storeroom look, making sure either that you stick to three colours at most, or that you go for all the colours of the rainbow for one glorious over-the-top colour effect.

ABOVE A walk-in cupboard is unusual today but always highly prized. Shelves line the walls and old and new china is grouped together according to shape.

RIGHT In a small kitchen, even shallow shelves, particularly when combined with sliding doors, can be used to store both china and glass.

HALLWAYS AND STAIRS

Although in many houses, the hall is frequently perceived of as narrow, this is often more a perception than an actuality. After all, there are few halls down which you actually have to sidle sideways, so on that basis I believe that if the hall is wide enough to walk down, then it is wide enough to find space for some storage. As you will see from what follows, there are decorative and storage opportunities in even the most unpromising of these spaces.

Obviously, any storage in such a high-traffic area as a hallway must be, if not unobtrusive, at the very least not an obstruction. To start with, most halls need storage space for coats and umbrellas. You will often find that there is room for a set of coat-hooks or pegs. The choice of styles and materials is wide, ranging from Shaker-type wooden pegs to brushed metal and you can choose from individual hooks to a row of hooks on some sort of decorative batten. You might even be lucky enough to find an old railway carriage coat rack in an antique shop. This will look great fixed to your hall wall, or perhaps you will come across an old-fashioned cast-iron coat stand with an umbrella holder beneath. The freestanding coat stand has made a comeback in recent years; one modern version looks like a traditional coat stand that has been cut in half lengthways so that it stands flat against the wall.

Bicycles – always a problem if you do not have a garden shed – are often left lying around in a hallway where they are dangerous and are certainly not things of beauty. These can be hung on wall brackets or you

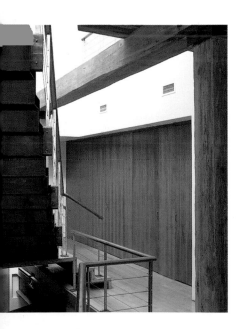

FAR LEFT In this narrow hall, an entire wall has been turned into one comprehensive storage unit, with veneered panels hiding both walk-in and racked storage.

LEFT A clever use of the tantalising space underneath the stairs combines both pull-out and open-out storage in a seamless, sleek design.

RIGHT In a mini-hall, two walls have been converted into striking storage that, although quite shallow, can hold a variety of things.

LEFT Against the wall beneath an open-tread metal staircase, a stepped, shelf unit wittily echoes the rise of the metal stairs.

RIGHT A beautifully designed and constructed piece of cabinetwork, this below-stairs storage combines cupboards and doors with a recessed drinks cabinet.

might find deep shelves with padded hooks beneath that are designed to hold a bike with your cycling gear on the shelf above.

But you may not want to have your possessions out on show, in which case you will need cupboards. Despite seeming narrow, halls often have enough space for shallow cupboards, even full-height cupboards if you want. And if space really is at a premium, you can always fit these cupboards with sliding doors.

There are still more hall-storage opportunities to be explored. Consider, for instance, the fact that most halls come with their architectural partner, the staircase. This offers the possibility of a clever beneath-

stairs storage area – a heaven-sent opportunity for the keen organiser. Storage ideas for such a space can vary from simple shelves cut to match the angled wall, through modular storage systems all the way to complex arrangements of tailor-made cupboards complete with flush doors that can make the whole storage area almost invisible.

Even the very stairs themselves can be converted into storage places. During the conversion of a small storage-light flat, one London architect took beneath-stairs storage a literal step further by converting the rise of each step into a shallow drawer in which a variety of small objects could be stored.

BEDROOMS

When it comes to questions of storage, there is a strong case for voting the bedroom the most important room in the house. We are always reading that the bedroom should be a haven of peace – somewhere to relax, unwind and shut out the busy, rushed world (and household) around. To achieve this it helps to have your bedroom things tidily stowed away. Chaos and calm do not good bedfellows make.

So what type of storage do we need? To answer this question you have to look carefully at your lifestyle and your wardrobe. People have such different modes of dress and ways of life that one man or woman's wardrobe is definitely not necessarily another's, and a man's storage requirements may be

THIS PAGE In this home, a dressing room is part of the bedroom and yet separate; designed to be in harmony with the sleeping quarters, the storage furniture is in the same simple style.

LEFT A clothes-storage unit in this pared-down bedroom is painted, below dado-height, in the same contrasting colours as the rest of the room.

different to a woman's. Does your life tend towards the formal or the
informal? Will you need therefore to have storage for traditional shirts or
casual tops, suits or tracksuits, dresses and skirts or trousers and sweaters?
Your answers will quickly show you what type of storage you need – shelves
for shirts and sweaters, tall hanging space for coats, dresses, trousers and
jeans, short hanging space for skirts, suits and tops, drawers or shelves for
underwear and socks, racks for shoes, boxes for hats. There are storage
solutions for all these wardrobe options and many more.

The next question to ask yourself is do you want built-in or freestanding
storage? Built-in storage is, as we have seen (see pages 38–47), also expensive
storage, but it does make it possible for every conceivable wardrobe whim to
be catered for. As with kitchen storage, there are bedroom storage systems
that have taken every possible combination of clothing into account: half and

THIS PAGE Although this vanity unit appears fitted, it is in fact freestanding; it contains both cupboards and drawers as well as the basin and integral mirror.

LEFT This pristine clothes storage is a large piece of furniture but instead of overshadowing the bedroom it fits in perfectly with the calm, white, almost clinical mood.

RIGHT No pretence is made here about the need for storage; in this room, a wall of walnut-veneered doors hides away everything that might need a home.

full hanging rails, slide-out trays, deep and shallow drawers, wire racks, shelves, hinged doors, sliding doors – any and every option is available.

Built-in storage has not had an altogether good press over the years. Many of us may still recall the 'fitted wardrobe' years – bedrooms dominated by a wall of flat, faceless doors, sometimes trimmed with strips of pointless moulding. But time and design have moved on. The best built-in systems today combine variety of design and materials in a way that truly enhances the mood and look of the room.

FLEXIBLE BEDROOM STORAGE

And then there are the more flexible – and usually less expensive – options of freestanding storage (see pages 52–59) or mobile storage (see pages 60–61). These allow you a certain open-mindedness about how and where you store

LEFT The traditional box-bed was a piece of ingenious design; warm and cosy in draughty old houses, it incorporated deep bed-depth drawers for storage of blankets and bed linen.

THIS PAGE In a very small but comfortable bedroom, the bedside table has been replaced by an over-the-bed oak shelf with discreet drawers for storing bedside essentials.

ABOVE In this attic bedroom built-in and freestanding storage are combined: along one wall are hardly-there built-in cupboards, while facing the bed, a pair of twentieth-century chests of drawers is both attractive and functional.

ABOVE RIGHT An antique chest of drawers has been given added importance in a small bedroom with the addition of an over-large bust and a dressing mirror arranged on the top.

your things, and of course you can move them around as you please or take them with you when you move, which may be an important consideration.

Contemporary freestanding storage encompasses bedroom-specific furniture such as fitted wardrobes or chests of drawers, but do not rule out old pieces. Many a useful piece for the bedroom sits unnoticed in an antique or junk shop. A judicious coat or two of paint, new door furniture and possibly a re-arrangement of the interior, and you will have a really useful, sturdy and commodious piece of bedroom storage. Or you might combine built-in with some freestanding pieces – a wall of hanging storage perhaps accompanied by a chest of drawers and a bedside table with shelves.

Falling somewhere between built-in and freestanding is modular furniture, comprising open-fronted boxes, boxes fitted with shelving or drawers, and boxes with doors on the front. These can be mixed and matched as you please and sometimes can be fixed to the wall. Generally speaking, modular furniture can only cope with the storage of small bedroom items such as clothing that can be stored flat or in drawers, music systems, books, CDs and DVDs, cosmetics and accessories such as handbags and jewellery. They offer, though, a useful, flexible alternative.

ABOVE In a small attic bedroom, low-level drawers along one wall and an angled wooden shirt hanger in the corner are clever storage solutions.

ABOVE RIGHT Large pieces in small spaces often have the effect of making a room seem larger; here, a traditional armoire adds scale and weight to this bedroom.

In a really small bedroom do not rule out lateral, or rather vertical, thinking. You might be able to raise your bed onto a platform, leaving the area below dedicated to storage and fitted with a combination of shelves, drawers and hanging space. Or, if you cannot raise your sights that high, think about storage space beneath a normal-height bed – perhaps some pull-out drawers on castors or drawers built into a divan base.

There are of course other bedroom storage solutions, from baskets and ottomans to plastic or wooden boxes on castors. You can also readily find expanding hanging rails as well as canvas storage systems with pockets to be hung from a door or hook. In addition, there are deep nylon 'hanging shelves' for sweaters and shirts as well as shallower versions for shoes.

Storage in children's bedrooms poses different problems. The more fun you can inject into it, the better. Clothes pegs on walls, hung at child-height, are a good way of encouraging a youngster to be tidy, as is a low chest of drawers, each with a picture showing what is inside. Another practical idea is a pair of low filing cabinets, spray-painted in cheerful colours and supporting a piece of board. This makes an excellent place for the child to draw, paint and play, with the equipment needed to hand in the cabinets below.

THIS PAGE The space at the end of the bed is often wasted; here it is taken up with a very simple open-fronted shelving unit with enough room for books and papers. The top surface provides a temporary resting place for other things but must be kept clear at bedtime.

Under-bed/end-of-bed/bedside

- In a larger room, there may be space to build a bedhead wall that can be made into a useful open shelf unit.

- Anything stored beneath the bed, whether in boxes or trays, must be covered to protect from dust.

- Look out for old wardrobe trunks in sales and junk shops for useful – and decorative – storage at the end or side of the bed.

Surprisingly your bed can be a source of extra storage. At either side, you could have a combination of shelf, table and drawers or cupboards, either in contemporary style or traditional – antique commodes make small, elegant cupboards. At the end of the bed, an open-fronted unit is useful for storing books and bits below and a television on top, or an ottoman could easily be fitted to hide a television which rises at the touch of a remote control button. Old chests or trunks are decorative and have enough room inside for bulky blankets and linen. If you do not have a bed with integral under-bed drawers, you can find many versions of useful, shallow, lidded storage boxes on castors that can be easily whizzed in an out – an important consideration at floor-level.

ABOVE In a simple bedroom with wooden floors and white walls, nothing could provide a degree of storage or look nicer than a traditional blanket chest, like this one in woven wicker, at the end of the bed.

RIGHT A modern take on a box-bed, this built-in bed has shelves in the wall behind and deep, wide drawers beneath.

BATHROOMS

Advances in technology and plumbing have changed the way that bathrooms look and work today, so much so that bathrooms are now considered as worthy of careful design, decoration and space planning as any other room in the house. And many bathrooms in homes built nowadays are smaller than they used to be. All of which means, of course, that bathroom storage must be taken seriously.

As elsewhere in the home, you have a choice of built-in or freestanding storage but the style you choose should generally be governed by where the bathroom is. If it is en suite with the bedroom, its style of decoration should echo that of the bedroom, giving a sense of the two spaces being connected. If you have a

separate bathroom, you can be more flexible, although probably, with a traditional home you will want a bathroom to match, and in a contemporary, home you might prefer a cutting-edge bathroom look.

Normally, the things that you want to store in a bathroom are divided into two very distinct types: those that you are happy to see and have seen at any time and those that you do not especially like to look at nor care for others to see. Into the first category come freshly laundered towels, decorative accessories and beautifully packaged lotions, potions and creams. In the second category are all those things that you need to have by you in the bathroom but which are for your and your maker's eyes alone.

OPPOSITE LEFT In this bright bathroom, cubbyholes have been built into the wall to hold decorative bathroom bits; below the basin unit are pull-out boxes for hidden-away storage.

THIS PAGE A double vanity unit in the form of a table provides storage for towels on polished wooden shelves that run the length of the entire unit.

OPPOSITE RIGHT In a small narrow bathroom, the best possible use has been made of the space by fitting deep drawers beneath the double basins.

SHELVES AND NICHES

For the things that you want to have on show, open storage is ideal. Glass or metal shelves are often chosen, since they are impervious to steam, but wood can also be used successfully as long as it is given a moisture-proof finish. Pretty bottles and jars look ethereal on glass shelves attached to the walls or across the window, while all those clean fluffy towels can be stored in the modern version of the traditional wash stand – a basin standing on or set into the top of a wooden cabinet, with a shelf or shelves below. In a traditional bathroom, an old-fashioned wash stand could still be used to house bottles, jars and towels if you wish.

If you are lucky enough to be planning a bathroom from scratch and are thinking of having a boxed-in bath, you might consider leaving room around it for a deepish shelf, either at one of the short sides, along the long side, or around both. Or you may have the chance to build some storage niches into the walls. These are especially useful in a small bathroom where you need to

ABOVE A freestanding vanity unit is compact and makes the best possible use of the space.

ABOVE LEFT Storage space in a small cloakroom is cleverly found In the false walls and in the boxing-in of the cistern.

RIGHT Under a ceiling of parquet tiles placed at angles to each other, a freestanding mid-twentieth-century storage unit echoes the warm tones of the curved bathroom furniture.

THIS PAGE A compact shower adjoining a sleeping area needs compact storage to match. Cubbyholes within the wall hold lotions and potions and are decorative as well as practical.

OPPOSITE A self-contained shower unit has the basin right next to the shower on a wooden countertop that echoes the wooden floor. Glass shelves on chrome supports, screened from splashes by the glass panel, provide useful storage for towels.

make use of every available bit of space. Both these solutions make attractive homes for items that can stand up to public scrutiny and, in a shower or alongside the bath, they can also provide a streamlined solution to the problem of where to keep the shampoo, shower gel or bubble bath.

Nor should you forget the simplest solutions – over-the-bath metal or wooden racks for the soap and sponge, wall-mounted or hanging racks in the shower.

OUT OF SIGHT, OUT OF MIND

To hide your less appealing bathroom items usually means built-in or freestanding furniture. If you have a small bathroom, do not assume that built-in is not for you. Many of today's systems are slimline and can actually make a small bathroom look larger.

Under-basin storage makes clever use of what would otherwise be wasted space and is a good place to store less-than-attractive cleaning materials. Choose from a cupboard with doors under the basin or perhaps some shelving to hold deep, unlidded boxes or baskets, the contents of which are, in effect, hidden from view.

Then there are low- or eye-level cupboards. If you choose a fitted furniture range, there may be a mirrored-front option for the eye-level cupboards .

Ottomans and stools that double as chests offer very useful dual-purpose storage, a mobile unit could be tucked away beneath the basin when it is not in use, and of course you may also want to have a lockable medicine cabinet in your bathroom.

But there are also less obvious bathroom spaces for this type of storage. If you have a concealed cistern, for example, the boxing-in can provide a shelf above or it can be extended to ceiling height and fitted with a push-catch door and interior shelves. Or you can make the whole or part of the bath panel into a hinged door

and use the space behind to store awkwardly shaped cleaning materials, toilet paper and other essentials.

Few houses still have the space for an old-fashioned linen cupboard, but perhaps you can fit in the modern version – a cupboard with sliding doors to maximise the space and slatted shelves to allow air to circulate. Or you could consider a small cupboard, built to fit in a corner, or a small version of the ubiquitous armoire, with the prettier linen on the upper, open shelves and the rest stored in the cupboard below.

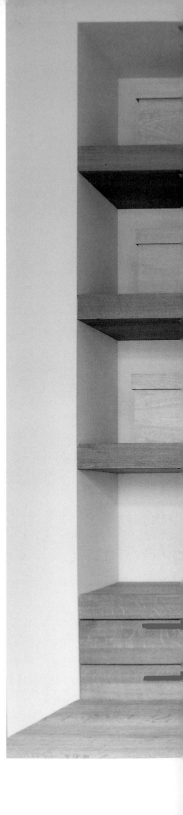

LEFT AND RIGHT In this rigorously disciplined home office, storage is built across the entire wall behind the desk. Shallow drawers run the length of the lower half, while the shelves above are furnished only with matching cardboard boxes, although other containers – metal boxes or woven baskets – would look equally striking. Each shelf is illuminated by a trio of recessed spotlights.

HOME OFFICE

One of the greatest changes in contemporary living is the advent of the home office – a space that might range from a complete, dedicated room to a miniscule corner too awkward to be used for anything else to a complete, dedicated room. Wherever you locate your home office, the sort of things you will need to store there are roughly the same: computer, printer, files, stationery and so on. And, as with storage solutions in other parts of the home, your choices range from built-in (see pages 38–47), through freestanding (see pages 52–59) to mobile (see pages 60–61).

But the location will, to some extent, determine the type of storage you use. For instance, if you only have a corner of the living room, you might choose the office-in-the-cupboard option – everything closed away behind space-saving sliding doors. Or you might prefer to make a feature of the office with a slick, contemporary wood or glass and metal work table or desk accompanied by an open shelving unit to store books and super-smart filing boxes. If your room is traditional in style, a dainty antique desk or table or the shabby chic version of the same, together with or incorporating a pretty shelf unit and some fabric-covered file boxes would fit the bill perfectly.

THIS PAGE A bedroom doubles as an office with a clever desk that has room for both office equipment and, on the pull-out shelf, personal belongings; the swing light can illuminate both desk and bed.

OPPOSITE LEFT Simple office storage that is highly effective; a functional unit holds filing boxes in perfect order.

OPPOSITE RIGHT This desk and its above-desk storage are designed to work as an integral part of the adjoining sitting area, both in function and style.

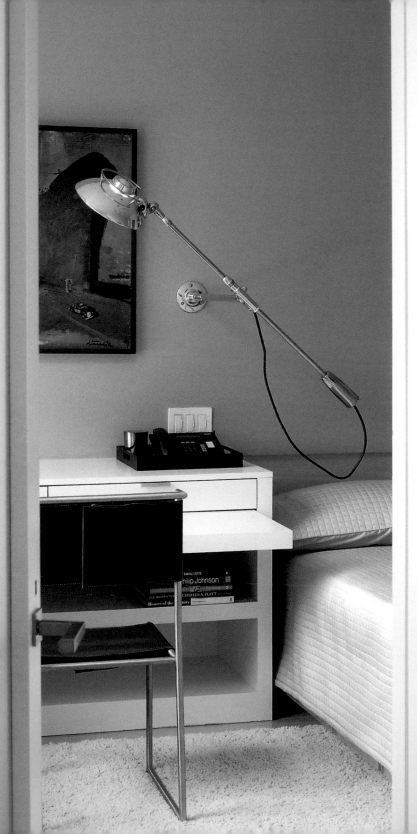

If you have no choice but to have your home office in the bedroom, your desk and shelving needs are the same but you might like to hide everything behind doors or a screen or curtain on the basis that it is not a good idea to go to bed – or wake up – with the next day's work staring you in the face.

When other potential office space has been sought – the area under the stairs, the creation of a mezzanine in a room with a high ceiling, the office as room divider (see page 50–51) – and there simply is nowhere to go, then that most mobile of home offices, the easy-gliding trolley might provide the answer. A good-sized example could easily hold a computer, printer and stationery and can be moved around as required.

And now to the detail of where to store all those files and stationery, for the office that conveys a sense of order is a delight, not only on a mental level but also on a practical one. Thankfully, the interest in home offices has meant the emergence of innumerable storage solutions. These include boxes, racks and trays in every shape, size and material from cardboard, printed fabric, wood and leather to plastic and metal. If you need full-size filing cabinets, these also now come in a huge range of materials to blend with every style – wood, metal, even basketweave. Or, if you like the look of 'salvaged style' there are many office solutions lurking in junk shops and at salvage merchants – old desks, filing cabinets and industrial shelving, are a few examples.

UTILITY ROOMS

If you are lucky enough to have a utility room, it is to be treasured. Most of us struggle to find somewhere to store the paraphernalia that is associated with laundry, cleaning and decorating.

As far as laundry appliances go, the best place to have them is anywhere but in the kitchen. Baskets of wet or dry clothes really don't work with food preparation and cooking. Once you begin to think about it though, there are, in fact, many alternative locations, ranging from in a bathroom, in a specially built cupboard in a cloakroom or along a corridor.

Washing machines and dryers can be stacked in a space-saving way as well as being installed in a row and there are now dryers that remove moisture through a condenser system rather than by being vented through a hose, so access to an outside wall is no longer an essential. A compact cupboard unit that houses vertically stacked appliances with shelves or a cupboard above the machines for clothes and linen can be fitted into a remarkably small space.

If you have the room, leave a corner free to stand a folded ironing board and to house a vacuum cleaner and bucket and mop, add a few more eye-level or low-level cupboards, some open shelves or an industrial-style storage system based on wall panels, shelving and drawers, and there you have your all-purpose utility room.

NO-ONE WANTS TO LIVE WITH THE WEEKLY WASH IN FULL VIEW, SO FINDING A SOLUTION TO THE PROBLEM OF STORING BOTH THE LAUNDRY AND THE WASHING AND DRYING APPLIANCES SHOULD ALWAYS BE A PRIORITY

ABOVE LEFT By stacking washing and drying machines and putting storage cupboards above and alongside, you can make a utility area out of the smallest space.

RIGHT Sometimes the old ways are best: a traditional rack on a pulley is ideal for drying and airing clothes. You can see how much storage can be packed into a tiny space.

Suppliers

GENERAL FURNITURE AND ACCESSORIES

AFTER NOAH
www.afternoah.com

ALFIES ANTIQUE MARKET
13–25 Church Street
London NW8 8DT
Tel: + 44 (0) 20 7723 6066
www.alfiesantiques.com

ALTERNATIVE PLANS
4 Hester Road
London SW11 4AN
Tel: + 44 (0) 20 7228 6460
www.alternative-plans.co.uk

ARAM DESIGNS
110 Drury Lane
London WC2B 5SG
Tel: + 44 (0) 20 7557 7557
www.aram.co.uk

AUTHENTICS
Tel: + 44 (0) 1932 871 305
www.authentics.co.uk

B & B ITALIA
www.bebitalia.it

B & Q
Portswood House
1 Hampshire Corporate Park
Chandlers Ford
Eastleigh SO53 3YX
Tel: + 44 (0) 845 609 6688
www.diy.com

BED BATH & BEYOND
Tel: +1-(800) 462-3966
www.bedbathandbeyond.com

BLISS
Tel: + 44 (0) 1789 400 077
www.blisshome.co.uk

THE BLUE DOOR
The Blue Door Yard
74 Church Road
London SW13 0DQ
Tel: + 44 (0) 20 8748 9785
www.thebluedoor.co.uk

BOCONCEPT
www.boconcept.com

CADIRA
www.contemporary-furniture-cadira.co.uk

CALIFORNIA CLOSETS
Tel: + 1-(888) 336-9709
www.calclosets.com

CATO
Centrespace
6 Leonard Lane
Bristol BS1 1EA
Tel: + 44 (0) 117 929 9977
www.cato-design.com

THE CHAIR COMPANY
16 Harben Parade
Finchley Road
London NW3 6JP
Tel: + 44 (0) 20 7722 8888
www.thechair.co.uk

CHAPLINS
477–507 Uxbridge Road
Hatch End
Pinner HA5 4JS
Tel: + 44 (0) 20 8421 1779
www.chaplins.co.uk

CHARLES PAGE
61 Fairfax Road
London NW6 4EE
Tel: + 44 (0) 207 328 9851
www.charlespage.co.uk

CONNECTIONS INTERIORS LTD
286–288 Leigh Road
Leigh-on-Sea
Essex SS9 1BW
Tel: + 44 (0) 1702 470939
www.connections.uk.net

THE CONRAN SHOP
Michelin House
81 Fulham Road
London SW3 6RD
Tel: + 44 (0) 20 7589 7401
www.conran.com

THE CONTAINER STORE
Tel: +1-(888) CONTAIN
www.containerstore.com

CRATE AND BARRELL
Tel: +1-(800) 967-6696
www.crateandbarrell.com

CRISPIN & GEMMA FURNITURE DESIGN
Faith House
12 Perseverance Works
238 Kingsland Road
London E2 8DD
TEL: + 44 (0) 20 7729 3838

www.crispinandgemma.com

DAVID LINLEY
60 Pimlico Road
London SW1W 8LP
www.davidlinley.com

DEBENHAMS
www.debenhams.com

DECORATIVE LIVING
55 New Kings Road
London SW6 4SE
TEL: + 44 (0) 20 7736 5623
www.decorativeliving.co.uk

DESIGNER FURNITURE
www.designerfurniture.co.uk

DESIGN ICONS LTD
The Coach House
Holly Street
Leamington Spa CV32 4TN
Tel: + 44 (0) 845 241 3500
www.designicons.co.uk

THE DESK COMPANY
16 Parson Street
London NW4 1QB
Tel: + 44 (0) 20 8203 2122
www.the-desk.co.uk

THE DINING ROOM SHOP
62–64 White Hart Lane
London SW13 0PZ
Tel: + 44 (0) 208 878 1020
www.thediningroomshop.co.uk

DISTINCTION FURNITURE AND INTERIORS
Bishops Park House
25–29 Fulham High Street
London SW6 3JH
Tel: + 44 (0) 207 731 3460
www.distinction-furniture.co.uk

DWELL
www.dwell.co.uk index.php

EASY CLOSETS
19 Chapin Road
Building D
Pine Brook, NJ 07058
Tel: +1-(800) 910-0129
www.easyclosets.com

ETHAN ALLEN
Tel: +1-(888) 324-3571
www.ethenallen.com

FRENCHY FURNITURE
1st Floor
63 Balham Hill

London SW12
Tel: + 44 (0) 20 8673 5019
www.frenchyfurniture.co.uk

FURNITURE123.CO.UK
www.furniture123.co.uk

FURNITURE CRAFT INTERNATIONAL LTD
www.fci.uk.com

FURNITURE DIRECT LTD
12 Scar Lane
Milnsbridge
Huddersfield
HD3 4PE
Tel: + 44 (0) 1484 648408
www.furnituredirectltd.co.uk

FURNITURE TODAY
Willow House
Green Hills Business Park
Tilford Road
Tilford GU10 2DZ
Tel: + 44 (0) 1252 793670
www.furnituretoday.co.uk

THE FURNITURE UNION
Bankside Lofts
65a Hopton Street
London SE1 9LR
Tel: + 44 (0) 207 928 5155
www.thefurnitureunion.co.uk

FURNITURE VILLAGE
www.furniturevillage.co.uk

GIGI LONDON
Tel: + 44 (0) 870 345 0640
www.gigilondon.com

GOTHAM
17 Chepstow Corner
1 Pembridge Villas
London W2 4XE
Tel: + 44 (0) 20 7243 0011
www.gothamnottinghill.com

GRAHAM & GREEN
4 & 10 Elgin Crescent
London W11 2HX
Tel: + 44 (0) 20 7727 4594
www.grahamandgreen.co.uk

GRAND ILLUSIONS
41 Crown Road
St Margarets
Twickenham TW1 3EJ
Tel: + 44 (0) 20 8607 9446
www.grandillusions.co.uk

HABITAT
www.habitat.net

HEAL'S
The Heal's Building
196 Tottenham Court Road
London W1T 7LQ
Tel: + 44 (0) 20 7636 1666
HOLD EVERYTHING
Tel: + 1-(800) 421-2264
www.holdeverything.com

THE HOLDING COMPANY
241–245 Kings Road
London SW3 5EL
Tel: + 44 (0) 20 7352 1600

HOME FRENZY
Unit 10
Evans Business Centre
Albion Way
Leeds LS12 2EJ
Tel: + 44 (0) 870 7200098
www.homefrenzy.com

HOWE
93 Pimlico Road
London SW1W 8PH
Tel: + 44 (0) 20 7730 7987
www.howelondon.com

IKEA
www.ikea.com

ILVA
Tel: + 44 (0) 845 245 8285
www.ilva.co.uk

INDIGO
275 New Kings Road
Parsons Green
London SW6 4R
Tel: + 44 (0) 207 384310
www.indigo-uk.com

ISOKON
Turnham Green
Terrace Mews
London W4 1QU
Tel: + 44 (0) 20 8994 7032
www.isokonplus.com

JOHN LEWIS
www.johnlewis.com

JOSEPHINE RYAN ANTIQUES
AND INTERIORS
63 Abbeville Road
London SW4 9JW
Tel: + 44 (0) 20 8675 3900
www.josephineryanantiques.co.uk

KOO DE KIR
65 Chestnut Street
Boston, MA 02108
Tel: +1-(617) 723-8111

www.koodekir.com
LAURA ASHLEY
Tel: + 44 (0) 871 9835 999
www.lauraashley.com

LEXTERTEN
14 Suffolk Avenue
Westgate-on-Sea CT8 8JG
Tel: + 44 (0) 1843 836888
www.lexterten.com

LILLIAN VERNON
Tel: +1-(800) 901-9291
www.lillianvernon.com

LOMBOK
Tel: + 44 (0) 870 240 7380
www.lombok.co.uk

MAISON DU MONDE
273–279 The High Street
London W3 9BT
Tel: + 44 (0) 20 868 00049
www.maisondumonde.com

MARK MAYNARD
651 Fulham Road
London SW6 5PU
Tel: + 44 (0) 20 7731 3533
www.markmaynard.co.uk

MARKS & SPENCER
www.marksandspencer.com

MODUS
Unit 5
Westcombe Trading Estate
Station Road
Ilminster TA19 9DW
Tel: + 44 (0) 1460 57465
www.modusfurniture.co.uk

MUJI
www.mujionline.co.uk

NEW HEIGHTS
www.new-heights.co.uk

NINA CAMPBELL FURNITURE
1–19 Chelsea Harbour Design
Centre
London SW10 0XE
Tel: + 44 (0) 20 7349 7577
www.ninacampbellfurniture.com

NORDIC STYLE
109 Lots Road
London SW10 0RN
Tel: + 44 (0) 207 351 1755
www.nordicstyle.biz

OKA DIRECT LTD
Unit 3A

Vogue Industrial Park
Berinsfield OX10 7LN
Tel: + 44 (0) 870 160 6002
www.okadirect.com

ONE DEKO
Old Spitalfields Market
111–113 Commercial Street
London E1 6BG
Tel: + 44 (0) 20 7375 3289
www.onedeko.co.uk

OPIUM
414 Kings Road
World's End
London SW10 0LJ
Tel: + 44 (0) 20 7795 0700
www.opiumshop.co.uk

PAPERCHASE
Tel: + 44 (0) 161 839 1500
www.paperchase.co.uk

PINE ON LINE
Malcolm House
2 Spring Villa Park
Edgware HA8 7EH
Tel: + 44 (0) 845 1080 183
www.pineonline.co.uk

POLIFORM
Tel: + 1(888) POLIFORM
www.poliformusa.com

PURVES & PURVES
Tel: + 44 (0) 20 8896 9972
www.purves.co.uk

ROOM SERVICE GROUP
www.roomservicegroup.com

SCP
135–139 Curtain Road
London EC2A 3BX
Tel: + 44 (0) 20 7739 1869

SELFRIDGES & CO
www.selfridges.com

THE SHOWHOME WAREHOUSE
11–17 Francis Court
Wellingborough Road
Rushden NN10 6AY
Tel: + 44 (0) 870 333 1556
www.showhomewarehouse.co.uk

SKANDIUM
86 Marylebone High Street
London W1U 4QS
Tel: + 44 (0) 20 7935 2077
www.skandium.com

SPACECRAFT
Morelands
5–23 Old Street
London EC1V 9HL
Tel: + 44 (0) 20 7253 5800
www.spacecraftint.com

SPACEMAKER
Paycocke Road
Basildon SS14 3DR
Tel: + 44 (0) 1268 441144
www.spacemakerfurniture.co.uk

STACKS AND STACKS
2665 Santa Rosa Ave.
Santa Rosa, California 95407
Tel: + 1-(800) 761-5222
www.stacksandstacks.com

THOMASVILLE
Tel: +1-(800) 225-0265
www.thomasville.com

WANT DONT WANT.COM
341 Euston Road
London NW1 3AD
Tel: + 44 (0) 20 7504 3456
www.wantdontwant.com

WILLIAM BALL
Tel: + 44 (0) 1375 375 151
www.wball.co.uk

ZINC DETAILS
2410 California Street
San Francisco, CA 94115
Tel: +1-(415) 776-9002
www.zincdetails.com

KITCHENS

ALNÖ
www.alno.co.uk

AYA KITCHENS AND BATHS
www.ayakitchens.com

CALLIER & THOMPSON
14180 Manchester Rd
St. Louis MO 63011
Tel: + 1-(636) 391-9099
www.calllerandthompson.com

HARVEY JONES KITCHENS
Tel: + 44 (0) 800 389 6938
www.harveyjones.com

JOHN STRAND (MK) KITCHENS
12–22 Herga Road
Wealdstone
Harrow HA3 5AS
Tel: + 44 (0) 20 8930 6006
www.johnstrand-mk.co.uk

KITCHEN ITALIA LTD
Unit 4
Spring Valley Business Centre
Porterswood
St. Albans AL3 6PD
Tel: + 44 (0) 800 093 9850
www.kitchenitalia.com

KRAFTMAID CABINETRY
P.O. Box 1055
15535 South State Ave
Middlefield, OH 44062
Tel: + 1 (440) 632-5333
www.kraftmaid.com

MAGNET
www.magnet.co.uk

NOLTE KITCHENS, INC
274 Bryan Rd.
Dania Beach FL 33004
Tel: + 1-(954) 929-0889
www.noltekitchens-usa.com

POGGENPOHL
477–481 Finchley Road
London NW3 6HS
Tel: + 44 (0) 207 435 5427

POLIFORM
Tel: + 1(877) VARENNA
www.poliformusa.com

UNPAINTED KITCHENS
258 Battersea Park Road
London SW11
Tel: + 44 (0) 20 722 32017
www.unpaintedkitchens.com

BEDROOMS

AND SO TO BED
Tel: + 44 (0) 808 144 4343
www.andsotobed.co.uk

BEDROOMFURNITUREUSA.COM
Tel: + 1-(866) 888-3058
www.bedroomfurnitureusa.com

BEDROOM FURNITURE DIRECT
(CSN STORES INC)
800 Boylston St
Suite 1600
Boston, MA 02199
Tel: + 1-(800) 311-4137
www.bedroom-furniture-
direct.com

CITY BEDS
Gibbins Road
London E15 1AH
Tel: + 44 (0) 800 026 3414
www.citybeds.co.uk

COUNTRY CHARM
468 Springfield Road
Rt. 133, Arcola, IL 61910
Tel: + 1-(888) 268-3355
www.countrycharmfurniture.com

COUNTY BEDS AND
BEDROOMS
Unit 1B
Denvale Trade Park
Haslett Avenue East
Crawley RH10 1SS
Tel: + 44 (0) 1293 526660
www.countybeds.com

FURNITURE TRADITIONS
www.furnituretraditions.net

THE LEATHER BED COMPANY
103 Wandsworth Bridge Road
London SW6 2TE
Tel: + 44 (0) 20 7731 3262
www.theleatherbedcompany.com

LITVINOFF & FAWCETT
281 Hackney Road
London E2 8NA
Tel: + 44 (0) 20 7739 3480
www.landf.co.uk

THE LONDON WALLBED
COMPANY
430 Chiswick High Road
London W4 5TF
Tel: + 44 (0) 20 8742 8200
www.wallbed.co.uk

TEMA CONTEMPORARY
FURNITURE
Tel: + 1-(80) 895-8362
www.temafurniture.com

WALLBEDS BY BERGMAN
1240 Calle De Commercio Unit J
Santa Fe, New Mexico 87507
Tel: +1-(800) 424-3634
www.wallbedsbybergman.com

BATHROOMS

THE ALBION BATH COMPANY
26 Hythe Quay
Colchester CO2 8JB
Tel: + 44 (0) 7000 422847
www.albionbathco.com

AMERICAN STANDARD
Tel: + 1-(800) 442-1902
www.americanstandard-us.com

BATHROOM LUXURY
65–69 High Street
Mansfield Woodhouse NG19 8BB

Tel: + 44 (0) 845 045 0068
www.bathroomluxury.co.uk

BATHROOM TRADING
COMPANY
40 Peterborough Road
Parsons Green
London SW6
Tel: + 44 (0) 20 7384 3570
www.bathroomtrading.com

BATHSTORE
www.bathstore.com
BOFFI
9 Hester Road
London SW11 4AN
Tel: + 44 (0) 20 7228 6460

BRITTEN'S BATHTIME
298–300 Baker Street
Enfield EN1 3LD
Tel: + 44 (0) 20 8342 0811
www.brittens-bathtime.com

COLOURWASH
18 Weir Road
London SW19 8UG
Tel: + 44 (0) 20 8944 2695
www.colourwash.co.uk

DOUG'S TUBS & MORE
Tel: + 1-(80) 991-2284
www.dougstubs.com

EYE DESIGN
30 Rectory Grove
Leigh-on-Sea SS9 2HE
Tel: + 44 (0) 1702 477 071
www.eyedesign.uk.com

GOODWOOD BATHROOMS
Church Road
North Mundham
Chichester P20 1JU
Tel: + 44 (0) 1243 532 121
www.goodwoodbathrooms.co.uk

HANSSEM
155 Helen St
South Plainfield, NJ 07080
Tel: + 1-(908) 754-4949
www.hanssemamerica.com

HERITAGE BATHROOMS
Princess Street
Bedminster
Bristol BS3 4A
Tel: + 44 (0) 117 963 3333

IDEAL STANDARD (UK) LTD
The Bathroom Works
National Avenue
Kingston Upon Hull HU5 4HS

Tel: + 44 (0) 1482 346461

IMPERIAL WARE
Unit 27
Gravelly Industrial Park
Thompson Drive
Erdington
Birmingham B24 8HZ
Tel: + 44 (0) 121 328 6824
www.imperialware.com/english
/co.asp

JUST ADD WATER
202–228 York Way
London N7 9AZ
Tel: + 44 (0) 20 7697 3161

KRAFTMAID CABINETRY
(see Kitchens)

ORIGINAL BATHROOMS
143–145 Kew Road
Richmond-upon-Thames TW9 2PN
Tel: + 44 (0) 208 940 7554
www.original-bathrooms.co.uk

PIPE DREAMS
Tel: + 44 (0) 207 225 3978
www.pipedreams.co.uk

ROCA LTD
Samson Road
Hermitage Industrial Estate
Coalville
Leicestershire LE67 3FP
Tel: + 44 (0) 1530 830 080

SHADES FURNITURE
Thorp Arch Estate
Wetherby LS23 7DD
Tel: + 44 (0) 1937 842 394
www.shadesfurniture.co.uk

TILES & BATHS DIRECT
60 The Broadway
London NW9 7AE
Tel: + 44 (0) 20 8202 2223

TOTAL BATHROOMS LTD
Brassmill Lane Trading Estate
Bath BA1 3JF
Tel: + 44 (0) 1225 462727
www.totalbathrooms.co.uk

THE WATER MONOPOLY
16–18 Lonsdale Road
London NW6 6RD
Tel: + 44 (0) 20 7624 2636
www.watermonopoly.com

HOME OFFICE

BLUE HEN OFFICE FURNITURE
116 S. Park Ave
Sanford, FL 32771
Tel: + 1-(888) 258-3436
www.bluehen.com

THE DESK COMPANY
16 Parson Street
London NW4 1QB
Tel: + 44 (0) 20 8203 2122
www.the-desk.co.uk

EUROTEK OFFICE FURNITURE
LTD
Southern Cross Trading Estate
Bognor Regis PO22 9SB
Tel: + 44 (0) 1243 868686
www.eof.co.uk

HOME WORKING SOLUTIONS LTD
500 Chiswick High Road
London W4 5RG
Tel: + 44 (0) 20 8956 2880
www.homeworkingsolutions.
co.uk

NATIONAL BUSINESS
FURNITURE
Tel: + 1-(800) 558-1010
www.nationalbusinessfurniture
.com

OFFICE FURNITURE2GO.COM
250 E. Wisconsin Ave
Milwaukee, WI 53202
Tel: + 1-(800) 460-0858
www.officefurniture2go.com

BESPOKE/CUSTOM FURNITURE

ALBAN INTERIORS
Unit 8
Willows Farm Village
Coursers Road
London Colney
St Albans AL2 1BB
Tel: + 44 (0) 1727 826265
www.albaninteriors.co.uk

ARTHUR BRETT
www.arthurbrett.com

ART WOODSTONE STUDIO
13852 Park Center Rd
Herndon VA 20171
Tel: + 1-(571) 323-2248
www.furniture.artwoodstonest
udio.com

BARRY COTTON ANTIQUES
116 Riverview Gardens
London SW13 8RA
Tel: + 44 (0) 208 563 9899

BOW WOW
Chapel Barton House
Bruton BA10 0AE
Tel: + 44 (0) 1749 812 500
www.bowwow.co.uk

BURCHWOOD USA
www.burchwoodusa.com
CARTER B. RICH
1751 Church St
Dalton NY 14836
Tel: + 1-(585) 476-2221
www.carterbrich.com

CRICK HOUSE INTERIORS
Weston Business Park
Weston on the Green OX25 3TJ
Tel: + 44 (0) 1869 343007
www.crickhouse.co.uk

DAVID JEST
166B Tower Bridge Road
London SE1 3LZ
Tel: + 44 (0) 20 7378 7933
www.davidjest.com

DAVID SALMON
1–19 Chelsea Harbour Design
Centre
London SW10 0XE
Tel: + 44 (0) 20 7349 7575
www.davidsalmon.com

DOMINIC ASH
Manor Farm Outbuildings
Manor Farm
Compton Abdale GL54 4DP
Tel: + 44 (0) 1242 890 184
www.dominicash.co.uk

DOMUS FURNITURE
6 & 7 Tilia Road
London E5 8JB
Tel: + 44 (0) 20 8525 0682

HABACHY DESIGNS INC
434 Marietta St, Loft 406
Atlanta, GA 30313
Tel: + 1-(404) 429-8878
www.habachydesigns.com

HORCHOW
Tel: + 1-(877) 944-9888
www.horchow.com

JALI LTD
Albion Works
Church Lane

Barham
Canterbury CT4 6QS
Tel: + 44 (0) 1227 833333
www.jali.co.uk

LENA PROUDLOCK
4 The Chipping
Tetbury GL8 8AA
Tel: + 44 (0) 1666 500 051
www.lenaproudlock.co.uk

LOUISE BRADLEY DESIGN
15 Walton Street
London SW3 2HX
Tel: + 44 (0) 20 7589 1442
www.louisebradley.co.uk

MODERNSPACES.COM
234 Townsend Street
San Francisco, CA
Tel: + 1-(415) 357-9900
www.modernspaces.com

STEVEN COLLINS CARPENTRY
Tel: + 44 (0) 20 8694 3777
www.stevencollinsltd.co.uk

WILLIAM YEOWARD
www.williamyeoward.com

WYNDHAM FURNITURE
7 Malthouse Drive
London W4 2NR
Tel: + 44 (0) 800 028 1384
www.wyndhamdesign.com

Architects & designers

1100 ARCHITECT
435 Hudson Street
New York
New York 10014
USA
Tel: + 1-(212) 645-1011
www.1100architect.com

ABRAHAM & THAKORE
LIMITED
D351 Defence Colony
New Delhi 110024
India
Tel: + 91 11 699 3714

ABSTRAKT ARCHITECTS
8 rue d'Enghien
75010 Paris
Tel: + 33 (0) 1 402 293 09

ADJAYE ASSOCIATES
23-28 Penn Street
London N1 5DL
Tel: + 44 20 7739 4969
www.adjaye.com

AGNÈS EMERY
12 rue de Lausanne
10060 Brussels
Belgium
Tel: + 32 (0) 2 538 2134
www.emeryetcie.com

ALEX VAN DE WALLE
Vlaamsesteenweg 3
1000 Brussels
Belgium
Tel: + 32 477 806 676
alex.vdw@swing.be

ANDREA TRUGLIO
75 via del Corso
00186 Rome
Italy
Tel: + 39 06 361 1836

ANDRÉE PUTMAN
83 avenue Denfert-Rochereau
75014 Paris
France
Tel: + 33 (0) 1 55 42 88 55
www.andreeputman.com

ANDREW WEAVING
Century Design
68 Marylebone High Street
London W1U 5JH
Tel: + 44 (0) 7487 5100

ANTHONY COCHRAN
Tel: + 1-(212) 529-1400
www.qcollection.com

ASFOUR GUZY ARCHITECTS
594 Broadway
Suite 1204
New York
New York 10012
USA
Tel: + 1-(212) 334-9350
www.asfourguzy.com

ATELIER D'ARCHITECTURE M
FRISENNA SCPL
15 rue de Verviers
4020 Liège
Belgium
Tel: + 32 (0) 4 341 5786

AUDREY MATLOCK
ARCHITECTS
141 West Broadway
New York

New York 10013
USA
Tel: + 1-(212) 267-2378
www.audreymatlock.com

AZMAN ARCHITECTS
18 Charlotte Road
Shoreditch
London EC2A 3PB
Tel: + 44 (0) 20 7739 8181
www.azmanarchitects.com

BLACK KOSLOFF KNOTT
ARCHITECTS
Level 9
180 Russell Street
Melbourne
Victoria 3000
Australia
Tel: + 61 (0) 3 9671 4555
www.b-k-k.com.au

BRUCE BIERMAN DESIGN INC
29 West 15th Street
New York
New York 10011
USA
Tel: + 1-(212) 243-1935
www.biermandesign.com

CHARLES RUTHERFOORD
51 The Chase
London SW4 0NP
Tel: + 44 (0) 20 7627 0182
www.charlesrutherfoord.net

COLLETT-ZARZYCKI
ARCHITECTS & DESIGNERS
Fernhead Studios
2b Fernhead Road
London W9 3ET
Tel: + 44 (0) 20 8969 6967
www.collett-zarzycki.com

CURTIS WOOD ARCHITECTS
23-28 Penn Street
London N1 5DL
Tel: + 44 (0) 20 7684 1400
www.curtiswoodarchitects.com

DAVID GILL GALLERY
3 Loughborough Street
London SE11 5RB
Tel: + 44 (0) 20 7793 1 100

DIAMOND BARATTA DESIGN INC
270 Lafayette Street
New York
New York 10012
USA
Tel: + 1-(212) 966-8892

DOMINIQUE PICQUIER
10 rue Charlot
75003 Paris
France
Tel: + 33 (0) 1 42 72 33 32
www.dominiquepicquier.com

DOWNTOWN GROUP
236 West 27th Street # 701
New York
New York 10001
USA
Tel: + 1-(212) 675-9506
www.downtowngroup.com

DRAKE DESIGN ASSOCIATES
315 East 62nd Street
5th Floor
New York
New York 10021
USA
Tel: + 1-(212) 754-3099
www.drakedesignassociates.com

EMMANUEL RENOIRD
4 rue de Phalsbourg
75017 Paris
France
Tel: + 33 (0) 1 45 56 99 24
www.emmanuelrenoird.com

ÉRIC GIZARD ASSOCIÉS
14 rue Crespin du Gast
75001 Paris
France
Tel: + 33 (0) 1 55 28 38 58
www.gizardassocies.com

FAHRENHEIT
130b Avenue Louise
1000 Brussels
Belgium
Tel: + 32 (0) 2 644 2800
www.fahrenheit.be

FEBO DESIGNS
Foxcombe
South Hartin
Petersfield GU31 5PL
Tel: + 44 (0) 1730 825041

FOUGERON ARCHITECTURE
431 Tehama Street
Suite 1
San Francisco
California 94103
USA
Tel: + 1-(415) 641-5744
www.fougeron.com

FRANÇOIS MARCQ
8 rue Fernand Neuray
1050 Brussels

Belgium
Tel: + 32 (0) 2 513 1328

FRED COLLIN
Bransdale Lodge
York YO62 7JL
Tel: + 44 (0) 1751 431137

FRÉDÉRIC MÉCHICHE
14 rue Saint Croix de la
Bretonnerie
75004 Paris
France
Tel: + 33 (0) 1 42 78 78 28

GALERIE YVES GASTOU
12 rue Bonaparte
75006 Paris
France
Tel: + 33 (0) 1 53 73 00 10
www.galerieyvesgastou.com

HALSTEAD DESIGNS
INTERNATIONAL
9 Warwick Square
London SW1V 2AA
Tel: + 44 (0) 20 7834 2511

HEIBERG CUMMINGS DESIGN
9 West 19th Street
3rd Floor
New York
New York 10011
USA
Tel: + 1-(212) 337-2030
www.hcd3.com

IPL INTERIORS
Dominique Lubar
Unit 28C1
Thames House
140 Battersea Park Road
London SW11 4NY
Tel: + 44 (0) 20 7622 3009

JAMES GORST ARCHITECTS
The House of Detention
Clerkenwell Close
London EC1R 0AS
Tel: + 44 (0) 7336 7140
www.jamesgorstarchitects.com

JAMES MOHN DESIGN
245 West 29th Street
Suite 504
New York
New York 10001
USA
Tel: + 1-(212) 414-1477
www.jamesmohndesign.com

JANE CHURCHILL FABRICS
www.janechurchill.com

Tel: + 44 (0) 20 8874 6484

JEAN-DOMINIQUE BONHOTAL
12 rue Alfred de Vigny
75008 Paris
France
Tel: + 33 (0) 1 56 79 10 80

JEAN-MARC VYNCKIER
49 rue Daubenton
59100 Roubaix
France
Tel: + 33 (0) 3 20 27 86 59

JOHANN SLEE
Slee Architects & Interiors 32
Pallinghurst Road
Westcliff 2193
South Africa
Tel: + 27 (0) 11 646 9935
johann@slee.co.za

JOHN BARMAN INC
500 Park Avenue
Suite 21a
New York
New York 10022
USA
Tel: + 1-(212) 838-9443
www.barman.com

JOHN PAWSON
Unit B
70-78 York Way
London N1 9AG
Tel: + 44 (0) 20 7837 2929
www.johnpawson.com

JOHNNY GREY LIMITED
Fyning Copse
Rogate
Nr Petersfield
Hampshire GU31 5DH
Tel: + 44 (0) 1730 821424
www.johnnygrey.com

KARI LALLALAINEN
Tel: + 358 (0) 9680 1828
kari.lappalainen@pp7.inet.fi

KARIM EL ACHAK ARCHITECT
7 rue de la Liberté
Marrakech
Morroco
Tel: + 212 (0) 44 44 73 13
associati@menara.ma

KARIM RASHID INC
357 West 17th Street
New York
New York 10011
USA
Tel: + 1-(212) 929-8657

www.karimrashid.com

KELLY HOPPEN INTERIORS
2 Munden Street
London W14 0RH
Tel: + 44 (0) 20 7471 3350
www.kellyhoppen.com

KRISTIINA RATIA DESIGNS
Tel: + 1-(202) 852-0027
kristiinaratia@aol.com

LAURENCE KRIEGEL
Originals Interieurs Design Corp
loladesign2002@yahoo.com

LEONARDO CHALUPOWICZ
3527 Landa Street
Los Angeles
California 90039
USA
Tel: + 1-(323) 660-8261
www.chalupowicz.com

MARC PROSMAN
ARCHITECTEN BV
Overtoom 197
1054 HT Amsterdam
The Netherlands
Tel: + 31 (0) 20 48 92 099
www.prosman.nl

MARK WILKINSON
Overton House
High Street
Bromham
Nr Chippenham
Wiltshire SN15 2HA
Tel: + 44 (0) 1380 850004
www.mwf.com

MARTIN BRUDNIZKI DESIGN
STUDIO
Unit 2N
Chelsea Reach
79-89 Lots Road
London NW10 0RN
Tel: + 44 (0) 20 7376 7555
www.mbds.net

MAXIME D'ANGEAC
ARCHITECTE
41 rue Puchet
75017 Paris
France
Tel: + 33 (0) 1 53 11 01 82

MIMMI O'CONNELL
Tel: + 44 (0) 20 7589 4836
moconnell@portofcall.com

NEXT ARCHITECTS
Weesperzijde 93
1091 EK Amsterdam
The Netherlands
Tel: + 31 (0) 20 463 0463
www.nextarchitects.com

OGAWA DEPARDON
ARCHITECTS
137 Varick Street # 404
New York
New York 10013
USA
Tel: + 1-(212) 627-7390
www.oda-ny.com

PAMPLEMOUSSE DESIGN INC
12 Charles Street
Suite 6D
New York
New York 10014
USA
Tel: + 1-(212) 741-0073
www.pamplemoussedesign.com

PAOLO BADESCO
Viale di Porta Vercellina 5
20123 Milan
Italy
Tel: + 39 (0) 24 100 737
www.paolobadesco.it

RIOS CLEMENTI HALE
STUDIOS
6824 Melrose Avenue
Los Angeles
California 90038
USA
Tel: + 1-(323) 634-9220
www.rios.com

SALLY SIRKIN LEWIS
J Robert Scott
500 North Oak Street
Inglewood
California 90302
USA
Tel: + 1-(877) 207-5136
www.jrobertscott.com

SEIBERT ARCHITECTS PA
325 Central Avenue
Sarasota
Florida 34236
USA
Tel: + 1-(941) 366-9151
www.seibertarchitects.com

SELLDORF ARCHITECTS
62 White Street
New York

New York 10012
USA
Tel: + 1-(212) 219-9571
www.selldorf.com

SETH STEIN ARCHITECTS
15 Grand Union Centre
West Row
London W10 5AS
Tel: + 44 (0) 20 8968 8581
www.sethstein.com

SHELTON, MINDEL &
ASSOCIATES
143 West 20th Street
New York
New York 10011
USA
Tel: + 1-(212) 243-3939

SMITH CARADOC-HODGKINS
ARCHITECTS
43 Tanner Street
London SE1 3PL
Tel: + 44 (0) 20 7407 0717
www.sch-architects.com

STEPHEN ROBERTS INC
Fourth Floor
250 West Broadway
New York
New York 10013
USA
Tel: + 1-(212) 966-6930
www.stephenroberts.com

STEVEN EHRLICH FAIA
10865 Washington Boulevard
Culver City
California 90232
USA
Tel: + 1-(310) 838-9700
www.s-ehrlich.com

STILES WILSON INC
83 Cocoanut Avenue
Sarasota
Florida 34236-5613
USA
Tel: + 1-(941) 366-8282

THAD HAYES DESIGN INC
80 West 40th Street
New York
New York 10018
USA
Tel: + 1-(212) 571-1234
www.thadhayes.com

THOMAS KJAERHOLM
Rungstedvej 86

2960 Rungsted Kyst
Denmark
Tel: + 45 (0) 45 76 56 56
www.kjaerholms.dk

TRISTAN AUER
5a Cour de la Métaine
75020 Paris
France
Tel: + 33 (0) 1 43 49 57 20
TUULA POYHONEN
Tuula.poyhonen@fonet.fi

VICENTE WOLF
333 West 39th Street
10th Floor
New York
New York 10018
USA
Tel: + 1-(212) 465-0590

WELLS MACKERETH
ASSOCIATES
Unit 14 Archer Street Studios
10-11 Archer Street
London W1D 7AZ
Tel: + 44 (0) 20 7287 5504
www.wellsmackareth.com

WHITE SENSE
Tegnergatan 9
113 40 Stockholm
Sweden
Tel: + 46 70 717 5700
www.whitesense.com

WILLIAM YEOWARD
270 Kings Road
London SW3 5AW
Tel: + 44 (0) 20 7349 7828
www.williamyeoward.com

Acknowledgements

Photographers' credits

Ken Hayden 16, 40 left, 42-43, 54-55, 73 right, 77 above right, 77 centre right, 77 below left, 80-81, 88-89, 114-115, 116-117, 130, 130-131

Vincent Knapp 126 right

Ray Main/Mainstreamimages 35, 124 left

Photozest/Inside/B Claessens 124 right, Photozest/Inside/H&L/J De Villiers 129

Lucinda Symons 46, 69 above

Frederic Vasseur 6 right, 34 left, 51 right, 52 above, 82 above, 86 right, 121, 133

Fritz von der Schulenberg 87 above,

Simon Upton 3 left & right, 4, 7, 11 centre left & right, 11 below left & right, 15 below, 19, 20, 21, 29 above left, 29 centre left & right, 29 below left & right, 30, 37 above & centre, 45, 47, 52 below, 53, 54, 55 below, 56, 57, 58, 64, 66, 68, 69 below, 70, 71, 76 centre left, 77, 82 below, 83, 86 left, 87 below, 94, 96 left, 96 below right, 98 below, 99, 103 above, 104-105, 105, 109 below, 112, 118, 120 right, 123 left, 123 right, 127

Alex Wilson 2, 11 above right, 72, 100 above left, 100 below left, 101

Andrew Wood 1, 3 centre, 5, 8-9, 11 above left, 12-14, 15 above, 17, 18, 22-27, 29 above right, 31, 32-33, 34 right, 37 centre right, 37 below, 38-39, 40 right, 41, 43, 44, 48, 49, 50, 51 left, 55 above, 59 60, 60-61, 62-63, 65, 67, 73 left, 74-75, 77 above left, 77 below right, 78-79, 82 below, 84-85, 90-91, 92-93, 95, 96 above right, 97, 98 above, 98 below, 100 above & below right, 102, 103 below, 106-107, 108, 110- 111, 113, 114, 116 left, 117, 119, 120 left, 122, 125, 126 left, 128, 132, 134-135

Location credits

2 designer Johnny Grey; 3 left designer David Gill; 3 centre designer Sally Mackereth of Wells Mackereth; 3 right a home featuring Jane Churchill fabrics; 4 a home featuring Jane Churchill fabrics; 5 Mr & Mrs Boucquiau's house in Belgium designed by Marina Frisenna; 6 right Nina Gustafsson's Swedish home; 7 Alex van de Walle's apartment in Brussels; 8-9 a house in Victoria designed by Black, Bosloff Knott; 11 above left Marina and Ivan Ritossa's Boffi kitchen designed by Alternative Plans; 11 above right designer Johnny Grey; 11 centre left Carefree & Figlar; 11 centre right a home featuring Jane Churchill fabrics; 11 below left a home featuring Jane Churchill fabrics; 11 below right Daniel Rozensztroch's apartment in Paris; 12 left Shane/Cooper residence, New York, designed by 1100 Architect; 12 right a house in Amsterdam designed by Marc Prosman Architecten BV; 13 Hilpert Residence, San Francisco designed by Ogawa Depardon Architects; 14 a house in Delhi designed by Abraham & Thakore; 15 above Richard & Lucille Lewin's kitchen designed by Seth Stein; 17 Tristan Auer's apartment in Paris; 18 an apartment in Paris designed by Abstrakt Architects; 19 Martine Colliander of White Sense's apartment in Stockholm; 20 designer Andrea Truglio, Rome; 21 Hanne Kjaerholm's house in Copenhagen, Denmark; 22 interior design by Stiles Wilson, Sarasota, Florida; 22-23 an apartment in New York designed by John Barman Inc.; 24 Marina and Ivan Ritossa's Boffi kitchen designed by Alternative Plans; 25 designer Fred Collin; 26-27 Catherine Chermayeff & Jonathan David's apartment in New York designed by Asfour Guzy; 30 Hanne Kjaerholm's house in Copenhagen, Denmark; 31 a penthouse loft in New York designed by Bruce Bierman Design Inc.; 32 Paolo Badesco's villa in Italy; 33 Marta Ventos's kitchen in Barcelona; 34 left David Berg's house in Sweden; 34 right an apartment in Belgium designed by Francois Marcq; 37 centre left designer Nathalie Hambro; 37 centre right Pam Skaist-Levy of Juicy Couture's house designed by Leonardo Chalupowicz; 37 below Marta Ventos's kitchen in Barcelona; 38 De Stad, Amsterdam designed by Next Architects; 38-39 a house in Italy designed by Paolo Badesco; 40 left designed by Thad Hayes Design, Inc.; 40 right a house in New York designed by Shelton, Mindel Associates; 40 right a house in New York designed by Shelton, Mindel Associates; 41 left Richard & Lucille Lewin's house in Plettenberg, South Africa designed by Seth Stein; 41 right Stark residence, London, designed by Curtis Wood Architects; 42-43 Patrick de Portere's apartment, designed by Andrée Putman; 43 James Gager & Richard Ferretti's New York designed by Stephen Roberts; 44 Susanna Colleoni & Didi Huber's home in Milan; 45 Vincente Wolf's apartment in New York; 47 Artists Ben Langlands and Nikki Bell's home in London; 48 Steven Ehrlich, FAIA's house in Venice, California; 49 left designed by Seibert Architects; 49 right Martin Harding's house designed by Audrey Matlock; 50 van Breestraat, Amsterdam designed by Marc Prosman Architecten BV; 51 left Anne Fougeron Architecture; 51 right Ben Cherner & Emma O'Neill's apartment in New York; 52 above Dominique Picquier's house in Paris; 52 below a home featuring Jane Churchill fabrics; 53 Daniel Rozensztroch's apartment in Paris; 54 Sarah Bredenkamp's apartment in London; 54-55 Andrzej Zarzycki's London home, design by Collett-Zarzycki; 55 above Kanetell Residence, New York designed by Downtown Group; 55 below Dominique Lubar of IPL Interiors' apartment in London; 56 left Laurent Dombrowicz & Franck Delmarcelle's house in Northern France; 57 Eric & Gloria Stewart's manor house in South West France; 58 David Gill's house in London; 59 designer Karim Rashid's apartment in New York; 60 Dean

Smith & Pearl Wou's home in London; 60-61 Jean-Marc Vynckier's home in Lille; 61 interior by Tuula Poyhonen; 62 left Mark Rios' kitchen in Los Angeles; 62 right a house in East Hampton designed by Selldorf Architects; 63 Laurence Kriegel's apartment in New York; 64 Alastair Gordon & Barbara de Vries home in New Jersey; 65 Gerhard Jenne's house in London, designed by Azman Owens Architects; 66 designer Lena Proudlock; 67 Mark Rios' home in Los Angeles; 68 William Yeoward's house in the country; 69 below Kanetell Residence, New York, designed by Downtown Group; 70 above left Jerry & Susan Lauren's apartment; 70 above right Agnès Emery's house in Brussels; 70 below a home featuring Jane Churchill fabrics; 71 Diane de Clercq's home in Rome; 72 designer Johnny Grey; 73 left Sara & Joe Farley's apartment in New York designed by Asfour Guzy; 73 right Patrick de Portere's apartment, designed by Andrée Putman; 74-75 Weaving/Thomasson Residence, London; 77 above left a house in East Hampton designed by Selldorf Architects; 77 above right Andrzej Zarzycki's London home, design by Collett-Zarzycki; 77 below left designed by Martin Brudnizki Design Studio; 77 below right Catherine Chermayeff & Jonathan David's apartment in New York designed by Asfour Guzy; 78 left Pam Skaist-Levy of Juicy Couture's house designed by Leonardo Chalupowicz; 78 right designed by Seibert Architects; 79 Weaving/Thomasson Residence, London; 80-81 Interior design by Jean-Dominique Bonhotal; 82 above Charles Rutherfoord & Rupert Tyler's London flat; 82 below an apartment in Paris designed by Frédéric Méchiche; 83 a house in France designed by Yves Gastou; 84-85 Martin Harding's house designed by Audrey Matlock; 86 left a home featuring Jane Churchill fabrics; 86 right Nina Gustafsson's Sweden home; 87 above designer Mimmi O'Connell; 87 below a home featuring Jane Churchill fabrics; 88-89 designed by Thad Hayes Design, Inc.; 90 Stark residence, London designed by Curtis Wood Architects; 91 Steven Ehrlich, FAIA's house in Venice, California; 92 left Marta Ventos' kitchen in Barcelona; 92 right Keith & Cathy Abell's New York house designed by 1100 Architect; 93 an apartment in Belgium designed by Francois Marcq, kitchen designed by Fahrenheit; 94 home of Peri Wolfman and Charles Gold in Bridgehampton; 95 left Peter Wheeler & Pascale Revert's London home, designed by Eric Gizard; 95 right Jamie Drake's apartment in New York; 96 left Yvonne Sporre's house in London; 96 above right Paolo Badesco's villa in Italy; 96 below right Martine Colliander of White Sense's apartment in Stockholm; 97 Mark & Cynthia Wilkinson's kitchen in Wiltshire; 98 above Dominique Kieffer's kitchen in Paris; 98 below Agnès Emery's house in Brussels; 99 home of Peri Wolfman and Charles Gold in Bridgehampton; 100 above left Mark & Cynthia Wilkinson's kitchen in Wiltshire; 100 above right Beatrice de Lafontaine's kitchen in Knokke, designed by John Pawson; 100 below left designer Johnny Grey; 100 below right Beatrice de Lafontaine's kitchen in Knokke, designed by John Pawson; 101 designer Johnny Grey; 102 left Kristina Ratia's Connecticut home; 102 right Antony & Kristen Smithie's kitchen designed by Amanda Halstead of Halstead Designs Intl,; 103 above Glen Senk & Keith Johnson's house in Philadelphia; 103 below Tony Baratta's house in Long Island; 104 Eric & Gloria Stewart's manor house in South West France; 104-105 Kate Dyson of the Dining Room Shop's house in London; 105 Lena Proudlock of Denim in Style's house in Gloucestershire; 106 A house in East Hampton designed by Selldorf Architects; 107 Evi Kalogianni Bouras' kitchen in London designed by Adjaye Associates; 108 Martin Harding's house designed by Audrey Matlock; 109 left Carefree & Figlar; 109 right designer Anthony Cochran, New York; 110 left Kanetell Residence, New York, designed by Downtown Group; 111 Illka apartment, Helsinki, designed by Kari Lappalainen; 112 Yvonne Sporre's house in London; 113 a house in Brooklyn, New York designed by Ogawa Depardon Architects; 114 Karim El Achak's house in Marrakech; 114-115 Andrzej Zarzycki's London home, design by Collett-Zarzycki; 116 left Illka apartment, Helsinki, designed by Kari Lappalainen; 116-117 designed by Sally Sirkin Lewis; 117 Stark Residence, London designed by Curtis Wood Architects; 118 Mr & Mrs Fasting's cabin in the Norwegian mountains, interior design by Heiberg Cummings Design; 119 Sally Mackereth & Julian Vogel's house in London designed by Sally Mackereth; 120 left Weaving/Thomasson residence London; 120 right Jerry & Maxine Swartz's house in Germantown, New York; 121 left designed by James Gorst; 121 right Nina Gustafsson's Swedish home; 122 Weaving/Thomasson Residence, London; 123 left Mr & Mrs Stokke's cabin the Norwegian mountains, interior design by Heiberg Cummings Design; 123 right Greville & Sophie Worthington's house; 125 an apartment in Belgium designed by Francois Marcq; 126 left Weaving/Thomasson Residence, London; 126 right designer Kelly Hoppen; 127 Emmanuel Renoird's house in Normandy; 128 Maxime & Athénais d'Angeac's home in Paris; 130-131 Jackie Villevoye's house in the Netherlands; 132 a penthouse loft in New York, designed by Bruce Bierman Design Inc.; 133 left Reed & Delphine Krakoff's Manhattan town house, designed by Delphine Krakoff of Pamplemousse Design Inc.; 133 right James Mohn & Keith Recker's apartment in New York, interior design as a collaboration between Keith Recker and James Mohn; 134-135 designer Lynn Fornieles of Febo Designs.

Writing a book can be a pain or a pleasure; in the case of this book, it was emphatically the latter, thanks to Jacqui Small's efficient, calm and organised team – Kate, Hilary, Ashley and Nadine – all of whom made Storage such an enjoyable and worthwhile project.